MOTIVATIONAL CLASSICS

Three Renowned Books
In One Volume

ACRES OF DIAMONDS

Russell H. Conwell

THE KINGSHIP OF SELF-CONTROL

William George Jordan

AS A MAN THINKETH

James Allen

CONTENTS

FORWARD

You are today the same you'll be five years from now, except for two things: the people you meet and the books you read. The people you meet can't always be with you, but what you read in books can remain with you a lifetime.

How often we hear of individuals who began a new era in their lives from the reading of a single book. Some books can touch every important area of our lives and make us better people. This small volume contains three such books...three reknown classics that could change your life dramatically.

Acres of Diamonds, a perennial favorite of mine, has a powerfully simple message which has helped millions of people recognize their potential for success. One of the most dynamic motivators of all time, Russell Conwell, promises if you will respond genuinely to the needs of humanity, you can find self-fulfillment "in your own backyard."

In *The Kingship of Self-Control*, William George Jordan leads you expertly along the road to personal triumph. Challenging us to cast away those facets of ourselves which cause us to be less than what we should be, Jordan points the way to ultimate growth and happiness through self-discipline.

One of the most enlightening books ever written, *As A Man Thinketh*, has been a personal favorite for decades. With insight and honesty, James Allen will inspire you to make your ideals become your reality. Having touched not only readers the world over, but me and my family as well, *As A Man Thinketh* is a book to be treasured.

Each of these classics was selected on the virtue of its message being one of timeless impact. From my own personal experience, I can say that they are books to which the individual will return again and again; for the principles they set forth will be as relevant tomorrow as they were more than half a century ago.

A single reading will start you moving toward your goals. A second reading will keep you on the track until you reach those goals. And a third reading (perhaps years from now), will make you smile in recognition of the truths you learned and were able to apply to your life.

Right here, you have everything you need to help make your life as tremendous as you've always wanted it to be. And right now, you have a brighter tomorrow ahead of you. Remember, you only get to keep what you give away and only enjoy what you have when you share it.

Tremendously,

Charles "T" Jones

6

ACRES OF DIAMONDS

by

Russell H. Conwell

About the Author

Russell H. Conwell (1843–1925), grew up believing in the infinite possibilities of mankind. His life was an example of that belief.

During his youth, the Conwell farm in Berkshire, Massachusetts, was a station for the Underground Railway and sheltered many a runaway slave. At the age of fifteen, Conwell, desiring to expand his horizons, worked his way to Europe on a cattle ship. Upon his return, he graduated from Wilbraham Academy where he had supported himself largely through his own exertions.

He was nineteen, an avowed atheist, and a law student at Yale when the Civil War began. Returning home to Massachusetts to raise a company of volunteer militia, he soon gained a reputation as a great recruiting officer and it was not long before he was elected captain of his own company.

He saw much action in battle and was appointed lieutenant-colonel before an event took place which changed his life. Severely wounded during a surprise Confederate attack at Kenesaw Mountain, Conwell was unable to stop his orderly from making a valiant attempt on his behalf. Sadly, while endeavoring to save his commander's life, the youth lost his own. Before he died, however, he spoke to Conwell of his Christian faith. So profound an effect did this have on Conwell, that he himself became a Christian.

After the war, he began a successful law practice and founded several newspapers. The death of his wife when he was twenty-nine, however, deepened his Christian faith, and he eventually joined the ministry.

Taking over an impoverished Baptist Church in Lexington, Massachusetts, he achieved remarkable success, and was ordained there in 1879. He afterwards accepted a call to the Grace Baptist Church of Philadelphia, which, under his leadership, flourished for many years and became the Great Baptist Temple in 1891.

Eventually, out of the night school in the church basement, with a corps of volunteer teachers, Conwell founded Temple University. To raise money to support the school, along with three hospitals which he also founded, Conwell became a prominent lecturer on a great variety of subjects, as well as the author of sixteen books. His most famous lecture, Acres of Diamonds, was given more than six thousand times during his life and is still proof today of his belief in man's limitless potential.

Acres of Diamonds

When going down the Tigris river in 1870, with a party of English travellers, I found myself under the direction of an old Arab guide, whom we'd hired at Bagdad to show us the ancient cities of Assyria. Although he was well acquainted with the land, he was one of those guides who felt it his duty to entertain us endlessly with stories.

So many tales did that old guide recount, that I grew weary of listening to him, and in order to get my attention at one point, he said to me, "Now I will tell you a story which I reserve for my particular friends!" Naturally, when he emphasized the words, "particular friends," I listened. And I have always been devoutly thankful that I did.

There once lived, not far from the river Indus, a Persian farmer by the name of Ali Hafed, the old guide began. Ali Hafed owned a very large farm with orchards, grain fields, and gardens. He was a wealthy, contented man—contented

11

because he was wealthy, and wealthy because he was contented.

One day the Persian farmer was visited by an ancient priest, one of the wise men from the East. He sat down by the fire and told Ali Hafed how this world of ours was made.

He said that the world was once a mere bank of fog, and that the Almighty thrust His finger into the fog and began slowly to move His finger around, gradually increasing speed until at last He whirled the bank of fog into a solid ball of fire. Then this ball of fire went rolling through the universe burning its way through other cosmic banks of fog, and condensing the moisture without, until it fell in floods of rain upon its hot surface, and cooled the outer crust. Then the internal flames burst through the cooling crust and threw up the mountains and hills, and made the valleys, plains and prairies of this wonderful world of ours.

When this internal, melted mass burst out and cooled very quickly, it became granite; that which cooled less quickly became silver; and less quickly, gold. And after gold, diamonds were formed. Said the ancient priest, "A diamond is a congealed drop of sunlight."

This is scientific truth. For a diamond is pure carbon—an actual deposit of energy from the sun.

The priest then declared that diamonds are the highest of God's mineral creations and that if Ali Hafed had one diamond the size of his thumb, he could purchase the whole country. If he had a mine of diamonds, he could place his children upon the thrones of countries throughout the world.

Ali Hafed, after hearing all about the great worth of diamonds, went to bed that night a poor man—poor because he was discontented, and discontented because he thought he was poor. "I want a mine of diamonds!" he said to himself, as he lay awake all night.

Early in the morning he sought out the priest. Shaking him out of his dreams, he asked, "Will you tell me where I can find diamonds?"

"Diamonds?" exclaimed the priest. "What do you want with diamonds?"

"I want to be immensely rich," replied Ali Hafed.

"Well then, go along and find them. That's all you have to do. Go and find them."

"But I don't know where to go."

"Well," said the priest, "if you will look for a river that runs over white sands between high mountains, in those sands you will always find diamonds."

"I don't believe there is any such river."

"Of course there is! In fact, there are plenty of them," said the priest. "All you have to do is go and find them."

Declared Ali Hafed, "I will go."

So he sold his farm, collected his money, left his family in the charge of a neighbor, and went off in search of diamonds. Beginning at the

Mountains of the Moon, he afterwards came around to Palestine, and then wandered on into Europe. At last, when his money was all spent, and he was in rags, hopelessly wretched and poverty-stricken, he stood on the shore of the bay of Barcelona, Spain, and watched the waves come rolling in. Then the poor, afflicted, suffering man cast himself into the oncoming tide, and sank beneath its foaming crest, never to rise again in this life.

My camel was suddenly brought to a stop by the old Arab guide, while he went back to fix the baggage on one of the other camels. Puzzled, I remember saying to myself, "Why does he reserve this story for his 'particular friends'?" There seemed to be nothing to it—one chapter and a hero quite dead.

When the old guide again took up the halter of my camel, he went right on with the story as though there had been no interruption. One day, the guide continued, the man who had purchased Ali Hafed's farm, led his camel out into the garden to drink. As the camel put its nose into the clear water of the garden brook, Ali Hafed's successor noticed a curious flash of light from the white sands of the shallow stream. Reaching into the water, he pulled out a black pebble having an eye of light that reflected all the colors of the rainbow. Finding the stone interesting, he took it into the house, put it on the mantel, and later forgot all about it.

Some days afterwards, he was visited by the

14

ancient priest, who, the moment he saw the flash of light from the mantel, rushed up to it and shouted, "Here is a diamond—here is a diamond! Has Ali Hafed returned?"

"No, no, Ali Hafed has not returned, and that is not a diamond. It is nothing but a stone I found right out here in the garden."

"But I know a diamond when I see one," declared the priest, "and I tell you this is a diamond!"

Together they rushed out to the garden stream and stirred up the white sands with their fingers, and lo! there came up other more beautiful and valuable stones than the first.

"Thus, was discovered the diamond mine of Golcanda," said the old Arab guide to me, "the most magnificent diamond mine in the history of mankind, exceeding even the Kimberly mine itself. The Kohinoor and the Orloff diamonds, belonging to the crown jewels of England and Russia, the largest diamonds on earth, came from that mine."

"Had Ali Hafed remained at home, and had he dug in his own garden, his cellar, and in his wheatfields, instead of undergoing wretchedness, starvation, poverty and death by suicide in a strange land, he would have had acres of diamonds. For every acre, yes, every shovelful of that farm afterwards, revealed gems which have decorated the crowns of monarchs."

After hearing the moral of his story, I saw why the old guide reserved this tale for his 'particular friends.' But of course I wasn't about to tell him I could see it. I wasn't because it was that old Arab's devious way of going around a subject, like a lawyer, saying indirectly what he did not dare say directly: that there was a certain young man then travelling down the Tigris river who might better be at home in America. No, I did not tell him I could see it.

Instead, I told him a story that was brought to mind by his tale. I told him of a man out in California in 1847, who owned a ranch. Hearing that gold had been discovered in Southern California, he sold his ranch to a Colonel Sutter, and he went off to search for gold, never to return again.

Colonel Sutter built a mill on the stream that ran through the ranch, and one day his little girl brought into the house some wet sand from the mill's raceway. She placed it before the fire to dry, and as she was sifting the sand through her fingers, a visitor noticed the first shining scales of real gold that were ever discovered in California.

Thirty-eight million dollars have been taken out of a very few acres since then, and the mine is not exhausted yet. In fact I've been told that a one-third owner of the mine has for years and years collected one hundred and twenty dollars in gold every fifteen minutes, sleeping or waking. Wouldn't you and I enjoy an income like that!

Yet a better illustration than that occurred

here in Pennsylvania. There was a man living here, not unlike some Pennsylvanians you know, who owned a farm, and he did with it what I would probably do with such a farm—he sold it. But before he sold it, he secured employment collecting coal oil for his cousin, who had his own business in Canada, where oil was first discovered on this continent.

At first, when the farmer wrote to Canada, his cousin had replied that he could not engage him because he knew nothing about the coal oil business. So the farmer, with commendable zeal, set himself to the study of the entire subject. Beginning with the second day of God's creation, when the world was thickly covered with rich vegetation, he studied how coal oil was formed. He studied until he knew all about it: where to find it, how to refine it, even what it smelled like and tasted like. So, when he wrote to his cousin for the second time, to tell him he knew everything that there was to know about the coal oil business, his cousin replied finally, "Well then, come ahead."

His farm sold for $833 (even money, no cents). And scarcely had he left for Canada, than the man who purchased the farm went out to attend to the watering of the cattle and discovered something curious. He discovered a plank across the stream in back of the barn, placed there by the previous owner. It was angled across the water, extending a few inches beneath the surface, in order to throw over to the opposite embankment a dreadful-looking scum through which the cattle would not put their noses. With the plank there, diverting the scum, the cattle could drink from a clear section of the stream.

The farmer who had gone to Canada had for twenty-three years been damming back a flood of coal oil, which state geologists declared later was worth hundreds of millions of dollars. The city of Titusville now stands there, on the land once owned by a man who had studied everything about coal oil from the second day of God's creation, up to the present time, and sold out for $833, no cents. And again I say, "No sense."

I have yet another illustration, this time from Massachusetts (I'm sorry to say, since that is where I grew up). A young man from Newburyport went to Yale to study mine engineering. He excelled to such degree that the university faculty began to employ him as a tutor for students who were behind in their mineralogy classes. During his senior year, he earned $15 a week as a tutor. When he graduated, his pay was raised to $45 a week and he was offered a professorship.

If they had raised that boy's pay from $15 to $15.60, he would have stayed and been proud of the place. But when they raised him to $45 at one shot, he went home to his mother and said, "What is $45 a week for a man with a brain like mine! Let's go out to California and stake out gold mines and get rich."

Since his mother was a widow and he was an

only son, he had his way. So they sold their homestead in Massachusetts, and instead of going out to California, ended up in Wisconsin, where he was employed by the Superior Copper Mining Company, for $15 a week with a contract that allowed him an interest in any mines he should discover for the company. To my knowledge, he never discovered any mines, neither did the company do well financially.

Back in Massachusetts, meanwhile, the farmer who had bought the old homestead, went out to dig potatoes. The potatoes had already been growing in the ground when he'd bought the place, so he filled a very large basket with them. As he was bringing the basket through the front gateway, the ends of the stone wall were so close together where they met at the gate, that the basket became stuck in the narrow opening.

In Massachusetts the farms are nearly all stone walls, and one is obliged to be economical with gateways in order to have someplace to put the stone. Setting the large basket on the ground, the farmer pulled it first on one side, then on the other, until he managed to squeeze it through the gateway. And as he was doing this, he noticed in the upper, outer corner of the stone wall, a block of native silver, eight inches square.

Now that professor of mines, mining and mineralogy, who knew so much about the subject that he would not work for $45 a week, had sat right on that silver when he'd made his bargain to sell that homestead. He'd been born and brought up there and had gone back and forth by that piece of silver, rubbing it with his sleeve until it could have cried out to him: "Here is a hundred thousand dollars, right here—come and take me!" But he would not take it. It was in a homestead in Newburyport, and there was no silver there. Silver was away off someplace else.

I often wonder what has become of him. I can imagine him out there in Wisconsin as he sits by his fireside, and says to his friends, "Do you know that man Conwell from Philadelphia?" "Oh yes, we've heard of him." "Do you know that man Jones?" "Yes, we've heard of him too." And there is laughter all around as he comments to his friends, "Well, they have done precisely the same thing I did."

And so the joke, my friends, is on us as well. For you and I have made the very same mistake. In fact, ninety out of every hundred people here have this very day made the same mistake.

I say to you that you have "acres of diamonds" right here in Philadelphia, where you are living now. "Oh," you might say, "you cannot know much about your city if you think there are any 'acres of diamonds' here." But who can say whether some person going down with his drill in Philadelphia won't find some trace of a diamond mine yet down there? How can you say you are not over one of the greatest diamond mines in the world?

But of course this simply serves to illustrate my thought: that if you don't have the actual diamond mine, you literally have all that the diamonds would be good for. You have the opportunity to get rich, to attain great wealth, here in Philadelphia, now. This is within reach of almost every man and woman who hears me speak tonight.

I have not come to this platform to recite something to you but to tell you what in God's sight I believe to be the truth: that the men and women gathered here tonight have within their reach 'acres of diamonds', opportunities to become vastly wealthy.

Never in the history of the world has a poor man without capital had such an opportunity to get rich quickly and honestly, as he has now in our city. And unless some of you get richer for what I am saying tonight, my time is wasted.

Yes, I say you ought to get rich. It is your duty to get rich. "But," say many of my pious brethren, "how can you, a Christian minister, spend time going up and down the country advising people to get rich, to give their time to getting money?" And some say, "Isn't it awful! Why doesn't he preach the gospel instead of preaching about man making money?"

Because I believe that to make money honestly, my friends, is to preach the gospel. And that the men who get rich may be the most honest men you will find in the community.

A young man, here tonight, said earlier, "I

have been told all my life that if a person has money he is dishonest, mean and contemptible." And I say, my friend, that is the reason why you have none—because you have that idea of people. The foundation of your faith is altogether false. Let me state clearly that ninety-eight out of one hundred of all the rich men in America are honest. That is why they are rich. That is why they are trusted with money. That is why they carry on great enterprises and find plenty of people to work with them. Because they are honest men.

Said another young man, "I hear sometimes of men that get millions of dollars dishonestly." Yes, of course you do, and so do I. But they are so rare that the newspapers talk about them all the time until you get the idea that all the other rich men got rich dishonestly. For a man to have money, even in large sums, is not an inconsistent thing. We preach against covetousness and use terms like "filthy lucre" so that Christians get the idea that when we stand in the pulpit we believe it is wicked for any man to have money—until the collection basket goes around and then we almost swear at people because they don't give more money. Oh the inconsistency of such doctrines as that!

Money is power and you ought to be reasonably ambitious to have it. I say this because you can do more good with money than you can without it. Money printed your Bible, money builds your churches, sends out your missionaries, pays your preachers—and you would not have many of them if you did not pay them. I am always willing that my church pay me a large salary. A man with a large salary can do more good with the power that is furnished to him, when his spirit is in the right place.

It is an awful mistake of pious people to think you must be poor in order to be righteous. Some men say, "Don't you sympathize with the poor?" Of course I do, or I would not have been lecturing all these years. However, the number of poor who are to be sympathized with is very small. To sympathize with a man whom God has punished for his sins, and help him when God would still continue a just punishment, is to do wrong. And we do that more than we help those who are deserving. While we should sympathize with God's poor—that is, those who cannot help themselves—let us remember there is not a poor person in the United States who was not made poor by his own shortcomings, or by the shortcomings of someone else.

A gentleman here asks me, "Don't you think there are some things in this world that are better than money?" Of course I do. We all know there are things more valuable than money. I know from a heart made unspeakably sad by a grave on which autumn leaves now fall. Yes, I know there are things higher, and sweeter and purer than money. Well does the man who has suffered know that there are things more sacred than gold. But tonight I am talking of money.

All of us know that love is the grandest thing on God's earth. But I say, fortunate is the lover who has plenty of money. For money has power, and in the hands of good men and women it can accomplish—it has accomplished—much good.

For a man to say, "I do not want money," is to say, "I do not wish to do any good for my fellowman." Religious prejudice is so great that some people think it an honor to be one of God's poor. I am looking in the faces of people who think just that way.

I heard a man say once in a prayer meeting that he was thankful he was one of God's poor. And I wondered what his wife thought about it, as she took in washing to support the household while he sat and smoked on the veranda. I don't want to see any more of that kind of God's poor. And I don't believe God wants to either.

Our era is prejudiced against advising a Christian man (or as a Jew would say, a Godly man), from attaining wealth, even though honorable, Christian methods are the only methods which sweep us quickly toward the goal of riches. I will give you an example of this prejudice. Years ago at Temple University, there was a young theological student who came into my office and said, "I feel it is my duty to come in and labor with you sir, for I have heard you speak about the desire for wealth being an honorable ambition, that it would make a man temperate, and industrious and anxious to have a good name. You said that man's ambition to have money would make him a good man. Yet, sir, the Holy Scriptures declare that money is the root of all evil."

I asked him where he had found that saying. And he replied that he found it in the Bible. So I asked him to go out into the chapel and get a Bible and show me where he had found it.

He went out and soon came stalking back with an open Bible, and all the bigoted pride of a narrow sectarian who founds his Christianity on some misinterpretation of Scripture. Placing the Bible before me on my desk, he fairly squealed into my ear, "There it is. You can read it for yourself."

I said to him: "Young man, when you get a little older you will learn not to trust another denomination to read the Bible for you. Though you belong to another denomination, you are taught in theological school that emphasis is exegesis. Now please take the Bible and read it yourself and give the proper emphasis to it."

He took the Bible and proudly read, "'The love of money is the root of all evil.'"

Then he had it right. And when one does quote aright from the Great Book, he quotes the absolute truth. "The love of money is the root of all evil." It is the worship of the means instead of the end. The man who worships the dollar instead of the purposes for which it ought to be used, the person who refuses to invest it where it will do the world good, the miser who hoards his money in his cellar, the man who hugs the dollar until the eagle squeals, has in him the root of all evil.

Think, if you only had the money, what you could do for your family, for your community, for your city. Think how you could endow Temple University yonder, if you only had the money and the disposition to give it. And yet my friends, people say that you and I should not spend time getting rich. How inconsistent it all is!

A young man came to me the other day and asked, "If Mr. Rockefeller is, as you think, such a good man, why is it everybody says so much against him?" Poor Mr. Rockefeller—the lies that are told about him because he has two hundred million dollars. So many people believe them. Yet, how false is the representation of that man to the world. When newspapers nowadays sell because of sensationalism, how little we can know what is true.

We have a prejudice against a rich man not only because of the lies that are told about him, but because he has gotten ahead of us. That is the whole of it—he has just gotten ahead of us. Why is Mr. Carnegie criticized so sharply by an envious world? Because he has gotten more than we have. If a man knows more than I know, am I not somewhat inclined to criticize his learning? And if a man stands in a pulpit and preaches to thousands, and I have fifteen people in my church who are all asleep, don't I criticize him? We all do that to the man who gets ahead of us.

26

I believe that when the man you are criticizing has one hundred million, and you have fifty cents, you both have just what you are worth. And if you get a hundred million, you will be criticized, and you will be lied about. For you can judge your success in any line by the lies that are told about you.

I say you ought to be rich. And, if I say that you should be rich, at least I ought to suggest how you can get that way. Now, some of you may say, "You don't know anything about business—you are a preacher." Well then, I will have to prove my expertise. I don't like to do this, but I must since my advice will not be accepted if I am not an expert.

My father kept a country store. If there is any place under the stars where a man gets all sorts of experience in every kind of mercantile transaction, it is in the country store. I am not proud of my experience, especially during the times when my father was away and he left me in charge of the store. Though, fortunately for him, this did not happen very often.

This is what occured many times during my father's absence. A man would come in the store and ask me, "Do you sell jackknives?" "No, we don't sell jackknives," I would reply, and then go off whistling a tune. What did I care about that man anyhow? Then a farmer would come in and ask, "Do you carry jackknives?" And I would reply, "No, we don't carry jackknives," and away I would go again whistling another tune without a care. Then a third man would come through the door and ask, "Do you sell jackknives?" "No," I would say, "why is everyone carrying on about jackknives? Do you think we keep this store just to supply the neighborhood with jackknives?"

The difficulty was that I had not learned then that the foundation of godliness and the principle of success in business are both precisely the same. The man who says, "I cannot carry my religion into business," advertises himself as either an imbecile in business, on the road to bankruptcy, or a thief. If he does not carry his religion into business, he will certainly fail within a very few years. Had I been running my father's store on a Christian plan, a godly plan, I would have had a jackknife for the third, or even the second customer when he called for it. Then I would have done him a service, and would have received a reward myself, which it would have been my duty to take.

There are some overpious Christians who think if you make a profit on anything you sell, you are an unrighteous man. On the contrary, you would be a criminal to sell goods for less than they cost. You have no more right to sell goods without making a profit on them, than you have to dishonestly overcharge a man beyond what the goods are worth. You should so sell each item that the person to whom you sell shall make as much as you do.

We should help our fellowman and get happiness from it. The man who goes home with the sense that he has stolen a dollar that day, that he has cheated a man out of his honest due, is not going home to sweet rest. He arises tired the next morning and goes to work with an unclear conscience. He is not a successful man at all, although he may have laid up millions.

But the man who has gone through life dividing always with his fellowman, making and demanding his own profits always with rights, and giving to others their rights and profits, lives every day content. This is the royal road to great wealth, and the history of hundreds of millionaires.

If you have a store in Philadelphia, and you are conducting your business just as I carried on my father's business in Worthington, Massachusetts, you are going by the wrong principle. If you care enough about your neighbors to take an interest in their affairs, to find out what they need, you should be a rich man. But you go through the world saying, "No opportunity to get rich," and there is the fault right at your own door.

Young men come to me who say, "I would like to go into business but I cannot because I have no capital." Capital! I say. Look at this wealthy generation living in Philadelphia, all of whom began as poor boys and you want capital to begin on?

The moment a young man gets more money than he has grown to by practical experience, that moment is cursed. It is no help to have a young man or woman inherit money. It is no help to your children to leave them money. But if you leave them education, if you leave them noble, Christian values, a wide circle of friends, and an honorable name, it is far better than money. Young men, if you have inherited money, don't regard it as help. For it will deprive you of the very best things in life. There is no class of people to be pitied so much as the inexperienced sons and daughters of the rich. I pity the rich man's son.

One of the grandest things a human heart can ever know is when a young man, who has earned his own living, takes his bride over the threshold of the door of the house he himself has earned, saved for and built, and he says with an eloquence greater than any language of mine, "I have earned this home myself. It is all mine. And I divide it with thee." That is one of the best moments in a human life.

A rich man's son cannot know that. He takes his bride into a finer mansion, perhaps, but he is obliged to say to his new wife, "My mother gave me this. My mother gave me that, and my mother gave me this," until his bride wishes she had married his mother.

Yes, I pity a rich man's son, unless he has the good sense of the elder Vanderbilt, which sometimes happens. He went to his father and asked, "Did you earn all your money?" Said the father, "I did. I began work on a ferryboat for twenty-five cents a day." Replied the son, "Then I will have none of your help." And he too tried to get employment on a ferryboat. Not finding work there, he obtained employment elsewhere for three dollars a week.

Now if a rich man's son will do that, he will get the discipline of a poor boy that is worth more than a university education. He would then be able to take care of his father's millions. Yet, as a rule, rich men will not let their sons do the very thing that made them great. They will not allow their sons to work. And the mother—why she would think it a social disgrace if her poor, little, lily-fingered boy had to earn his living with honest toil.

So I say to the young men who complain about a lack of opportunity because they have no capital: Be glad of it! If you have no capital, be happy. What you need is common sense, not copper cents.

Look at A.T. Stewart, who started life as a poor boy in New York. He had $1.50 in his pocket when he went into the mercantile business. And 87 ½ cents of that dollar and a half he lost on his first venture, because he bought some needles and threads and buttons to sell which people did not want. So he had the goods left on his hands, a dead loss.

A.T. Stewart learned the great lesson of his mercantile career. He decided: "I will never buy anything more until I first learn what the people want." That one thing is the secret to success. It matters not what your profession or occupation in life may be; whether you are a lawyer, a doctor, a housekeeper, teacher or whatever else, the principle is precisely the same—you must first know the demand. Learn first what people need and then invest yourself where you are most needed. Success is almost certain to follow.

A.T. Stewart then went around to people's doors and asked them what they wanted, and when he found out, he invested his 62 ½ cents to supply a known demand. On that principle, he went on to become a millionaire. His fortune was made by losing something, which taught him a great lesson. When will you salesmen learn it? When will you manufacturers learn that you must know the changing needs of humanity if you would succeed in life? Apply yourselves, all you Christian people, as merchant or manufacturer or workman, to supply that human need.

Another favorite illustration of mine is John Jacob Astor, who came across the sea so penniless, he was in debt for his fare. Yet that poor boy, with nothing in his pocket, made a fortune on this very same principle. He illustrated what can be done anywhere.

Early on in his career, he held a mortgage on a millinery store. Because the people there could not sell enough bonnets to pay the interest and the rent, he foreclosed the mortgage, took possession of the store and went into partnership with the very same people, in the same store, with the same capital. He left them alone in the store to do business as they had done before and then went out and sat down upon a bench in the park. To my mind he had the most pleasant part of that partnership, for as he sat on that bench, he was watching all the ladies as they went by. And what man wouldn't get rich at that business?

As he sat on that park bench, every time a lady passed by, he would study her bonnet. And before that bonnet was out of sight, he knew the shape of the frame, the color of the trimmings, the curl of the feathers. So then he went back to the store and said, "Put in the window just such a bonnet as I describe to you, because I have seen a lady who likes such a style." Then off he went again to sit on the park bench. Other ladies passed him with different bonnets. He returned to the store again, and told his partners what else to make for the shop window, until he filled his window with hats and bonnets the likes of which he knew the ladies already wanted. And a tide of customers immediately began to come in, making his shop the foundation of one of the greatest stores in New York.

Yes, A.T. Stewart went on until he was worth forty million, and John Jacob Astor's fortune is even greater. "But a man could make a fortune in New York," I can hear some of you say, "not here in Philadelphia." My friends, have you ever read the statistical account gathered in New

York in 1889, of the 107 millionaires worth over ten million? It is remarkable that people think they must go there to get rich. Out of those 107 millionaires, only seven of them made their money in New York. The others all moved to New York after their millions were made. Sixty-seven of them made their fortunes in towns of less than 6,000 people. And the richest man in the country today has never moved away from his hometown of 3,500 inhabitants. If you can get rich in New York, or anywhere else, you can certainly get rich in Philadelphia. It is not so much where you are, my friends, as what you are.

Look at the poor carpenter from Hingham, Massachusetts. Out of work, he was lounging around the house, when his wife told him to go out and find something to do. So he went out and sat down by the bay and whittled a soaked shingle into a wooden chain. His children quarreled over it that evening and so he whittled another one to keep the peace. While he was whittling, a neighbor came by and said, "Why don't you make some toys, if you can carve as well as that?" "Oh," replied the carpenter, "I wouldn't know what to make." "Why don't you ask your own children?" suggested the neighbor. "What's the use of trying that? My children are different from other people's children."

Nevertheless, the next morning he asked his daughter, "What would you like for a toy?" And she told him she would like a doll's carriage, a doll's umbrella, a doll's bed, a doll's washstand, and went on with a list that would take a lifetime to supply. So after consulting his own children in his own house, he took the firewood, for he had no money to buy lumber, and began to whittle those strong, unpainted Hingham toys that for years have been known all over the world. He is now one of the richest men in Massachusetts.

I remember a man from up in my native hills; a poor man who for forty years owned a widespreading maple tree that covered his poor cottage like a benediction from on high. In the spring the man would put spouts in the tree and catch the maple sap in buckets. One day he made the maple sugar from that tree so white and crystalline that a visitor was so impressed he suggested the old man sell it for confectionary. The old man took the advice and invented "rock maple crystal". Before the patent expired, he had ninety thousand dollars and had built a beautiful mansion near the site of that tree.

After forty years owning that maple tree, he awoke to find it had a fortune in it. And many of us are right by the tree that has riches for us. We own, and do what we will with it, but we do not learn its value, for we do not see the human need we could be filling with it.

If I went through this audience tonight and asked you to introduce me to the great inventors here, you would probably shrug in reply, not realizing that a great inventor sits next to you, or that you are such a person yourself. Did you ever study the history of invention and see how strange it is that the man who made a great discovery did it without any previous idea that he was an inventor?

Look at the poor man in Massachusetts who worked in a nailworks factory until he was injured at the age of thirty-eight. Afterwards, he could only earn a little money employed in the office to rub out marks on invoices made by pencil memorandums. He used a piece of rubber until his hand grew tired. Then one day he tied a bit of rubber on the end of a stick so he could work it like a plane. When his little girl came to see him she said, "Why you have invented something haven't you?" So the man went to Boston and applied for a patent, and every one of you that has a rubber-tipped pencil in your pocket, is now paying tribute to him. Not a penny did he invest—no capital at all. And yet he made millions.

Who are the great inventors? They are persons with plain, straightforward, common sense, who have seen a need in the world and applied themselves to supply that need.

I was lecturing in New Britain, Connecticut, and a lady who had been in the audience went home afterwards and tried to take off her collar. But the collar button stuck fast in the buttonhole. Fed up with buttons, she announced, "I am going to make something better to put on collars." Whereupon her husband made fun of her, saying, "After what Conwell said tonight, you should be able to make a great fortune."

When her husband ridiculed her, this woman made up her mind she would make a better collar button—and she did. She invented the snap button, which you can find everywhere now. And she went into partnership with several manufacturing firms and now has enough money to go over the sea every summer in her own private steamship—and yes, she even takes her husband with her.

I tell you the same message tonight, that she heard me tell years back: your wealth is too near you. You are looking right over it. Of course she had to look over it because it was right under her chin.

A man who heard that very same message in a lecture I gave in North Carolina, sat in the audience directly behind a lady who wore a large hat. When I said, "Your wealth is too near you, you are looking right over it," he whispered to his friend beside him, "Well, then, my wealth is in that hat." He wrote to me later telling me that he drew up a plan for a better hat pin than was in the hat of the lady sitting before him. The pin is now being manufactured and he was just offered fifty-two thousand dollars for his patent. That man made his money before he got out of that lecture hall.

Who are the great inventors? They are men and women like yourselves who probably think you could not invent anything. I can hear you saying now, especially you women, "How can we make a fortune when we are stuck in some shop, or in a laundry, or running a sewing machine, or working a loom?" Yet you have all heard of Mrs. Jacquard have you not? She invented the Jacquard loom that wove every stitch you are wearing. And Mrs. Greene invented the cotton gin, the machine which transformed the South. She showed the idea to Mr. Whitney, and he, like a man, seized it. So little credit has been given to Mrs. Greene. And do you know who invented the sewing machine? Elias Howe, you say? Well let me tell you the real story.

Elias Howe was in the Civil War with me and often in my tent telling of how he worked fourteen years to put together a sewing machine. His wife finally told him that they were going to starve to death if there wasn't something or other invented soon. At last she took matter into her own hands and one day, in two hours time, she invented the sewing machine. Of course Elias took out the patent in his name. Men do that sort of thing.

Who invented the mower and the reaper? According to Mr. McCormick's recently published report, it was a West Virginia woman. A woman also invented the trolley switch. And according to Mr. Carnegie, a woman invented the great iron squeezers which laid the foundation for the steel industry in the United States. Now if women can invent such things, we men should be able to invent anything under the stars! I say that for the encouragement of all you men.

The great inventors are simple people, just like the rest of us. Did you ever know a really great man? His ways are so simple and common, so plain, that you would think anyone could do what he is doing. A great man's friends and neighbors do not regard him as so great because they see that he is just like everybody else.

When I set out to write the biography of General Garfield, one of the grandest men of the nation, I was surprised when one of his neighbors took me around to his back door and shouted, "Jim, Jim!" And very soon General Garfield came to the door and let me in. To his neighbor he was just plain, ordinary, "Jim."

Down in Virginia some years ago, I went to an educational institution and was directed to a man who was out planting a tree. Approaching him, I asked, "Could you possibly direct me to the President of the University, General Robert E. Lee?" The man replied, "Sir, I am General Lee." Despite his noble reputation, he was a plain and simple man.

At the end of the Civil War, I had to go to Washington to see the President concerning one of my soldiers who had been sentenced to death. In the waiting room of the White House, I sat on benches with a lot of other people as the secretary asked one after another what they wanted. At last he got around to me and I was shown into the anteroom. "That is the President's door right over there," the secretary told me. "Just rap on it and go in."

I was never so taken aback in my life as the secretary went out and left me to face the President's door alone. I had been on fields of battle where bullets hit me and shells shrieked past me, but even Antietam was not so frightening as that moment. I don't know how I mustered up the courage to approach the door and, at arm's length, tap on it—but I finally did. The man inside was no help to me at all, for he yelled out, "Come in and sit down."

Abraham Lincoln's greatness lay in one principle which he always followed: whatsoever he had to do, he put his whole mind to it and kept it there until the thing was done. When I walked into that room, he stuck to the papers at his desk and did not look up at me, while I sat on the edge of a chair, trembling. Finally, when he had put a string around his papers, and pushed them to one side, he looked over to me and a smile came to his worn face. "I am a very busy man and have only a few minutes to spare," he said. "Now tell me in the fewest words what it is that you want."

I brought up the case of my soldier. "I have heard all about it," Mr. Lincoln said. "You need not say more. You may rest assured that the President never signed an order to shoot a boy under twenty years of age, and never will. You can tell that to his mother."

Then he asked me, "How has it been going in the field?"

"We sometimes get discouraged," I replied.

"It is very near the end, we are going to win now. I will be glad when it is through. No man ought to wish to be President of the United States. When I am finished here, Tad and I are going to Springfield. I bought a farm out there and I don't care if I earn only twenty-five cents a day. Tad has a mule team and we're going to plant onions. Were you brought up on a farm?"

"Yes," I said. "In the Berkshire Hills of Massachusetts."

He threw his leg over the side of his big chair and said, "I have heard many a time, ever since I was young, that up there in those hills you have to sharpen the noses of the sheep in order for them to get down to the grass between all the rocks." He was so familiar, so everyday, and farmer-like, that I right away felt at home with him.

He then took hold of another sheaf of papers and looking at me, said, "Good morning." Taking the hint then, I got up and went out, hardly able to believe that I had just seen the President of the United States.

A few weeks after, I was in the White House again, as part of the crowd passing through the East Room, by the coffin of Abraham Lincoln. When I looked at the upturned face of the murdered President, I felt that here was one of the greatest men God ever raised up to lead a nation

41

on to liberty. And he was such a simple man; a plain man.

When the second funeral was held, I was invited, among others, to see the coffin put in the tomb in Springfield, Illinois. Around the tomb stood Lincoln's old neighbors. To them he was just "Old Abe."

Who are the great men and women of our country today? They are simple people, exactly like you, my friends, sitting in this audience tonight, here in Philadelphia. Great men do not necessarily have to be presidents, or hold some office, as is the popular belief today. We must realize that men are great only on their intrinsic value, and not on the position they may happen to occupy.

Certainly great men get into office sometimes, but this nation is governed by the people, for the people, and the office-holder is but the servant of the people. The Bible says that the servant cannot be greater than the master. "He that is sent cannot be greater than He who sent him." In this country the people should be the masters and the office-holders should be honest servants of the people.

Great men do not necessarily have to fight in a war, or become war heroes who march up to the cannon's mouth, amid glistening bayonets, to tear the enemy's flag from its staff. It is no evidence of true greatness for a man to come home from battle with stars on his shoulders.

I remember a Peace Jubilee here after the

Spanish-American War. Some of you saw the procession go up Broad Street. My family wrote me that the tally-ho coach with Lieutenant Hobson upon it, happened to stop in front of our house. All the people threw up their hats and swung their handkerchiefs and shouted, "Hurrah for Hobson!" Had I been there, I would have yelled too, since Hobson deserves more from this country than he has ever received. But if I asked a high school class tomorrow, "Who sunk the Merrimac?" and the answer came back "Hobson," they would be telling me seven-eighths of a lie. For there were eight men who sunk the Merrimac. There were seven other heroes, who by virtue of their position, were continually exposed to the Spanish fire, while Hobson, as an officer might reasonably have been behind the smokestack.

I do not believe I could find a single person here tonight who could name the other seven men who were with Hobson. We ought to realize that however humble the position a man occupies, if he does his full duty, he is just as much entitled to the American people's honor as is a king upon his throne.

One last illustration I will give you, is one I wish I could leave out. If you go to the library to read this lecture, however, you will find this has been printed in it for twenty-five years. But for that fact, I would leave it out. Nevertheless, I will close my eyes now and go back in time to my native town in Massachusetts, in 1863. I can see the cattle-show ground filled with people, the town hall crowded, and the flags flying. I can hear the bands playing and the people shouting. Well do I recall that moment.

Everyone had turned out to receive a company of soldiers which was marching up on the Common. They had served out one term in the Civil War and re-enlisted, and were now being paid tribute by their townsmen. I was but a boy, but I was captain of that company and puffed out with pride. Why a cambric needle would have burst me all to pieces.

We marched into the town hall through a great throng of people, and while my soldiers took seats in front of the assembly, I, to my surprise, was invited by the mayor to come up on the platform with all the town officers. When I had taken my seat, feeling like Napolean the Fifth, and all had become silent throughout the hall, the mayor stepped forward. Everyone supposed that he would introduce the Congregational minister, the only orator in the town, who would give the oration to the soldiers.

You should have seen the surprise that ran through the audience when they discovered that the mayor, who was an old farmer, was going to deliver the address himself. He had never made a speech before in his life, but he fell into the same error that hundreds of other men have fallen into: he thought that his office should make him a great orator.

He had written down a speech and probably

walked up and down the pasture, frightening the cattle while he learned it by heart. Pulling his manuscript out of his pocket, he spread it carefully on the table, adjusted his spectacles, and assumed an elocutionary attitude.

His speech began: "Fellow citizens..." Upon hearing the sound of his own voice, he began to shake and tremble all over. After choking and swallowing, he began again: "Fellow citizens, we...are...we are...we are...we are...we are very happy...we are very happy...we are very happy...to welcome these soldiers who have fought and bled...and come back again to their native town. We are especially...we are especially...we are especially pleased to see with us today this young hero (which meant me)...this young hero...who in imagination (remember friends that he said, "in imagination," for certainly I would not be egotistical enough to mention this otherwise), who in imagination we have seen leading...we have seen leading...leading...we have seen leading his troops into the deadly breach. We have seen his shining...his shining...we have seen his shining sword...flashing in the sunlight as he shouted to his troops, 'Come on!'"

Oh dear, how little that good, old man knew about war. If he had known anything, he would have been aware that it is a crime for any officer of the infantry to go ahead of his men in time of danger. Officers must stay behind the line in actual battle, not because they are any less

45

brave, but because that is one of the laws of war. If a general came up to the front line, for instance, and he was killed, you would lose your battle, because he has the battle plan in his head, so he must be kept in comparative safety.

There sat in the hall that day, men who had given me their last bite of rations, who had carried me on their backs across the deep rivers of the Carolinas. The speaker mentioned them briefly, yet they were little noticed, although they too had fought for a cause they believed to be right.

And there were some men who should have been there, but were not. For they had gone to their deaths for their country. Yet, I, a mere boy, was the hero of the hour. Why? Simply because the mayor had fallen into the human error of putting an officer above the soldiers.

I learned a lesson then that I will never forget so long as the bell of time continues to ring for me. Greatness consists not in holding some office, but in doing some great deed with little means. Greatness is the accomplishment of vast purposes from the private ranks of life.

He who believes in the opportunities that are right here, where he lives, he who can give to his people better schools and colleges, more churches, better streets and sidewalks, more happiness and more of God, will be great anywhere. He who cannot be a blessing where he now lives, will never be great anywhere on the face of God's earth.

Let every man and woman here tonight begin where you are now, with what you are. Whether you work on a farm, in a factory, or behind the counter in a store, whether you keep house, or whatever is your station in life, remember that true greatness and its rewards are the priceless products of a genuine response to humanity's needs. And the opportunities to meet those needs, those "acres of diamonds," are in your own back yard.

THE KINGSHIP
OF SELF-CONTROL

by

William George Jordan

About the Author

William George Jordan (1864–1928), formed his convictions on self-discipline early in life. His great popularity came from his expression of those convictions, which are as relevant today as they were at the turn of the century.

Jordan began his literary career at the age of twenty. Instead of graduating from the College of the City of New York, he left to become the editor of two different literary magazines.

A keen interest in educational reform caused him to withdraw for a time from editorial work, in order to lecture on "Mental Training." His talent for writing, however, soon prompted his return to the literary world, where in 1894, he became the managing-editor of the Ladies' Home Journal, and later of the Saturday Evening Post.

Imbued with a strong sense of social justice, Jordan observed the need for a greater uniformity in state legislation throughout the country. So, in 1907, he proposed the organization of state executives into a House of Governors. His proposal led President Roosevelt to take action, and the first meeting of the actual House of Governors was held in 1910.

During this time, his series of homilies, commenced in 1899, began bringing Jordan national acclaim. *The Kingship of Self-Control,* his first in the series, bears a message that has touched the lives of thousands and reveals its author as a man whose ideals were noble both in precept and in practice.

I

The Kingship
of Self-Control

Man has two creators—his God and himself. His first creator furnishes him his raw material and his moral conscience with which he can make of his life what he will. His second creator, himself, has marvelous powers he rarely realizes. It is what a man makes of his capacities that counts.

When a man fails in life, he usually says, "I am as God made me." When he succeeds, he proudly proclaims, "I am a self-made man." Man is placed into this world not as a finality, but as a possibility. His greatest enemy is himself. In his weakness, man is the creature of circumstance. In his strength, he is the creator of circumstance. Whether he be victim or victor depends largely upon himself.

Man is never truly great merely for what he is, but ever for what he may become. Until he is filled with the knowledge of his possibility, and with the realization of his privilege to live the life for which he is individually responsible, he is merely groping through the years.

To see his life as he might make it, man must go up alone into the mountains of spiritual thought as Christ went alone into the Garden; leaving the world in order to gain strength to live in the world. There he must breathe the fresh, pure air of the recognition of his divine importance as an individual. Then, with a mind cleansed and invigorated, he must approach the problems of his daily living.

Man needs less of the "I am a feeble worm of the dust" element in his theology, and more of the concept: "I am a great human soul with marvellous possibilities." With such an affirmative view of life, he may see how to attain his kingship through self-control—the same type of self-control that is seen in the simplest phases of daily living, differing only in degree. This control, man can attain, if only he will. It is but a matter of paying the price.

The power of self-control is one of the great qualities that differentiates man from the lower animals. He is the only animal capable of a moral struggle or a moral conquest.

Every step in the progress of the world has been a new "control." It has been an escape from the tyranny of a fact, to the understanding and mastery of that fact. For ages man looked in terror at the lightning flash. Today he understands it as electricity, a force he has mastered and made his slave. The million phases of electrical invention are but manifestations of our control over a great force. Yet, the greatest of all "control" is man's self-control.

At each moment of man's life he is either a King or a slave. As he surrenders to a wrong appetite, to any human weakness; as he falls prostrate in hopeless subjection to any condition, to any environment, to any failure, he is a slave. Alexander the Great conquered the whole world except himself. Emperor of the earth, he was a servile subject of his own passions.

As man daily crushes out human weakness, masters opposing elements within, and day by day recreates a new self from the sin and folly of his past, then he is a King. He is a king ruling with wisdom over himself.

We look with envy upon the possessions of others and wish they were our own. Sometimes we feel this in a vague way with no thought of real attainment, as when we wish we had another's crown or self-satisfaction. Othertimes, however, we grow bitter, storm at the wrong distribution of the good things of life, and then lapse into a hopeless, fatalistic acceptance of our condition.

We envy the success of others, when we should emulate the process by which that success was achieved. We see the splendid physical development of Sandow, yet forget that as a babe and child he was so weak that there was little hope his life might continue.

We envy the power and spiritual strength of a Paul, without recollecting the weak Saul of Tarsus from whom he was transformed through his self-control. Thousands of instances of the world's successes—mental, moral, physical, financial, or spiritual—came from beginnings far weaker and poorer than our own.

Any man may attain self-control if he only will. He must not gain it, however, except by continued payment of price, in small, progressive expenditures of energy. Nature has an installment plan for each individual. No man is so poor that he cannot begin to pay for what he wants from life. And every small, individual payment that he makes, Nature accumulates for him as a reserve fund of strength in his hour of need.

The mental, physical and moral energy man expends in daily right-doing and in bearing the little trials of his daily life, Nature stores for him as a wondrous reserve so he may overcome any crisis of life. Nature never accepts a payment in full for anything. This would be an injustice to the poor and to the weak. Nature only recognizes the progressive installment plan.

No man can make a habit in a moment, or break it in a moment. It is a matter of development, of growth. But at any moment man may *begin* to make or begin to break any habit. This view of the growth of character should be a stimulus to the man who sincerely desires and determines to live nearer to the limit of his possibilities.

Self-control may be developed in precisely the same manner as we tone up a weak muscle: by a little exercise each day. Let us, daily, do as mere exercises of discipline in moral gymnastics, a few acts that are disagreeable to us; the doing of which will help us in instant action in our hour of need. The exercises may be very simple: dropping for a time an intensely interesting book at the most thrilling page of the story, jumping out of bed at the first moment of waking, walking a mile or two when the temptation is to take the car, talking to a disagreeable person and trying to make the conversation pleasant. These daily exercises in moral discipline will have a wondrous effect on man's whole moral nature.

The individual can attain self-control in great things only through self-control in little things. He must study himself to discover what is the weak point in his armor, what is the element within him that keeps him from his fullest success. This is the characteristic upon which he should begin his exercise in self-control. Is it selfishness, vanity, cowardice, morbidness, temper, laziness, worry, mind-wandering, lack of purpose? Whatever form human weakness assumes in the masquerade of life, he must discover it. He must then live each day as if his whole existence were telescoped down to the single day before him. With no useless regret for the past, no useless worry for the future, he should live that day as if it were his only day, the only day left for him to assert all that is best in him, the only day left for him to conquer all that is worst in him.

He should master the weak element within him at each slight manifestation from moment to moment. Each moment then must be a victory for it or for him. Will he be King, or will he be slave? The answer rests with him.

II

The Crimes of the Tongue

The second most deadly instrument of destruction is a loaded gun. The first is the human tongue. The gun merely kills bodies. The tongue kills reputations and oftentimes ruins characters. Each gun works alone; each loaded tongue has hundreds of accomplices. The havoc of the gun is visible at once. The full evil of the tongue lives through all the years and beyond what a man might see in his lifetime.

The crimes of the tongue are words of unkindness, of anger, of malice, of envy, of bitterness, of harsh criticism, gossip, lying and scandal. Theft and murder are awful crimes, yet in any single year the aggregate sorrow, pain and suffering they cause in a nation is microscopic when compared with the sorrows that come from the crimes of the tongue. Place on one side of the scales of Justice all the evils resulting from the acts of criminals, and on the other side all the grief, tears and suffering resulting from the crimes of respectablity, and you will stare in amazement as you see the scale you thought the heaviest shoot into the air.

At the hands of thieves or murderers few of us suffer, even indirectly. But from the careless tongue of a friend, the cruel tongue of envy, who is free? No human being can live a life so true and pure as to be beyond the reach of malice, or immune from the venom of envy.

The insidious attacks against one's reputation, the loathsome innuendos, slurs, half-lies by which jealous mediocrity seeks to ruin its superiors, are like parasitic insects that kill the heart and life of a mighty oak. So cowardly is the method, so stealthy the shooting of the poisoned thorns, so seemingly insignificant each separate act, that one is not on guard against them. It is easier to dodge an elephant than a microbe.

In London they once formed an Anti-Scandal League. The members promised to combat in every way possible "the prevalent custom of talking scandal, the terrible and unending consequences of which are not generally estimated."

Scandal is one of the crimes of the tongue responsible for moral contagion. Every individual who breathes words of scandal is punished by Nature: the eyes are dimmed to sweetness and purity, the mind is deadened to the glow of charity. There develops an ingenious perversion of mental vision by which every act of others is explained and interpreted from the lowest possible motives. Like carrion flies, scandalous tongues pass lightly over acres of flowers to feast on a piece of putrid meat. A keen scent is developed for the foul matter upon which to feed.

Noble hearts are broken in the silence whence comes no cry of protest. Gentle, sensitive natures are seared and warped. Old friends are separated and made lonely. Cruel misunderstandings deaden hope and make all life look dark. Such are a few of the sorrows that come from the crimes of the tongue.

A man may lead a life of honesty and purity, battling bravely for all he holds dearest, so sure of the rightness of his life that he never thinks for an instant of the diabolic ingenuity that makes evil report where only good really exists. A few words lightly spoken by the tongue of slander, a significant expression of the eyes, a cruel shrug of the shoulders, and then friendly hands grow cold, the accustomed smile is replaced by a sneer and a good man stands alone with a dazed feeling of confusion, wondering what has caused it all.

This craze for scandal is largely due to the sensational media of today. Each broadcast or printing is not one tongue, but thousands, often a million, telling the same wretched story to as many pairs of listening ears. The vultures of sensationalism can smell the carcass of immorality from afar. Collecting from the uttermost parts of the earth, the sin, disgrace and folly of humanity, they bare it all to the world. They do not even require *facts,* for morbid memories and fertile imaginations make even the worst of the world's happenings seem tame when compared with the monstrosities of invention. These stories, and the discussions they excite, develop in readers a cheap, shrewd power of distortion of all human deeds taking place around them.

If a rich man gives a donation to some charity, they say, "He is doing it to get his name talked about; to help his business." If he gives it anonymously, they say, "Oh, it's some millionaire who is clever enough to know that refraining from giving his name will pique curiosity; he will see that the public is informed later." If he does not give to charity, they say, "He's stingy with his money, of course, like all millionaires." To the vile tongue of gossip and slander, Virtue is deemed but a mask, noble ideals but a pretense, and generosity a bribe. The man who stands above his fellows must expect to be the target for the envious arrows of their inferiority. It is part of the price he pays for his advance.

One of the most detestable characters in all literature is Shakespeare's Iago. Envious of the promotion of Cassio over him, he hated Othello. His was one of those low natures that becomes absorbed in sustaining his dignity, talking of "preserving his honor," forgetting it has so long been dead that even embalming could not preserve it. Day by day, with studied vengeance, Iago distilled the poison of distrust and suspicion into more powerfully insidious doses. With a mind concentrated on the blackness of his purpose, he wove a network of circumstancial evidence around the pure-hearted Desdemona, and then murdered her at the hand of Othello. Her very simplicity, self-confidence and artless innocence, made Desdemona the easier mark for the diabolical tactics of Iago.

Iago still lives in the hearts of thousands who have his despicable meanness without his cleverness. The constant dropping of their lying words of malice and envy have in too many instances worn away the noble reputations of those superior to them.

To sustain ourselves in our own hasty judgments, we sometimes accept without investigation the words of these modern Iagos: "Well, where there is so much smoke, there must be some fire." Yet we forget that the fire may be lit by the torch of envy, thrown into the innocent facts of a superlative life.

III

The Red Tape of Duty

Duty is the most over-lauded word in our vocabulary. It is the cold, bare anatomy of righteousness. While duty looks at life as a debt to be paid, love sees life as a debt to be collected. Duty is ever paying assessments, whereas love is constantly counting premiums.

Duty is forced, like water through a pump. Love is spontaneous, like a mountain spring. Duty is prescribed and formal; it is part of the red tape of life. It means running on moral rails. Good enough as a beginning, it is poor as a finality.

The boy who stood on the burning deck and committed suicide on a technical point of obedience, has been held up to school children as a model of faithfulness to duty. He was placing, however, the whole responsibility for his act on someone outside himself. A victim of blind adherence to the red tape of duty, he was helplessly waiting for instruction in the hour of emergency, when he should have acted for himself. His act was an empty sacrifice. It was a useless throwing away of a human life. It did no good to his father, the ship, the nation, or himself.

The captain who goes down with his ship, when he has done everything in his power to save others, and when he can save his own life without dishonor, is the victim of a false sense of duty. He is cruelly forgetful of the loved ones on the shore whom he is sacrificing. His death means a spectacular exit from life, the cowardly fear of an investigation committee, or a brave man's loyal, but misguided sense of duty. A human life, with its wondrous possibilities, is too sacred to trust to be thus lightly thrown into eternity.

They tell us of the "sublime nobleness" of the Roman soldier at Pompeii, whose skeleton was found centuries afterwards, imbedded in the lava which swept down upon the doomed city. He was still standing at one of the gates, at his post of duty, still grasping a sword in his hand. His was a morbid faithfulness to a responsibility from which he was released by a great convulsion of nature. Like an automaton he stood, just as long, just as boldly, and just as uselessly.

The man who gives one hour of his life in living, consecrated service to humanity is doing greater work in the world than an army of Roman sentinels paying useless tribute to the red tape of duty. There is to be, of course, no sympathy for the man who deserts his post when he is needed. This is but a protest against losing the essence of true duty by worshipping the mere form of it.

Analyze any of the great historic instances of loyalty to duty, and wherever they ring true, you will find the presence of the real element that made the act almost divine. It was no mere sense of duty that made Grace Darling risk her life in a fierce storm of night, on a raging sea, to rescue the survivors of the wreck of the "Forfarshire." It was the sense of duty made real by a love of humanity. It was the heroic courage of a heart filled with divine compassion.

Duty is a hard, mechanical process for making men do things that love would make easy. It is a poor understudy to love and too low a motive for inspiring humanity. While love is the soul, duty is the mere shell. Love can transmute all duties into privileges, all responsibilities into joys.

The workman who drops his tools at the stroke of twelve, as suddenly as if he had been struck himself, may be doing his duty, but nothing more. No man has made a great success of his life, or a fit preparation for immortality, by doing his mere duty. He must do that, and yet still more. If he puts love into his work, the "more" will be easy.

The nurse may watch faithfully at the bedside of a sick child because it is her duty. But to the mother's heart, the care of the little one in the battle against illness, is never a duty. The mantle of love thrown over every act makes the word "duty" have a jarring sound, like the voice of desecration.

When a child turns out badly in later years, the parent may say, "Well, I always did my duty by him." Small wonder the boy turned out poorly. "Doing his duty by his son," too often implies merely food, lodging, clothes and education by the father. Why a public institution would offer that! What the boy needed most was deep draughts of love, and an environment of trust, counsel and sympathy. The parent should be an unfailing refuge, a constant resource and inspiration, not a mere larder, or hotel, or school that furnishes these necessities free. The empty boast of mere parental duty is one of the dangers of modern society.

Christianity stands forth as the one religion based on love, not duty. It sweeps all duties into one word—love. What duty creeps to laboriously, love attains in a moment. Duty is not lost, condemned or destroyed in Christianity; rather it is dignified, purified and exalted. All its rough expressions are made smooth by love.

The supreme instance of generosity in the world's history is not the giving of millions by some great name, it is the giving of a mite by some poor person whose name is never acknowledged. And behind that person's mite was no sense of duty, but rather the desire to give freely of a heart filled with love. Hundreds of times in the Bible the word "love" is mentioned. "Duty" is mentioned but five times.

In the conquest of any mental or moral weakness, in the attainment of any strength, as well as in our truest relation to ourselves and to the world, let us make "love" our watchword, not mere "duty." In our desire to live a life of honesty, we must not expect to keep to the narrow line of truth under the constant lash of duty's whip. Let us begin to love the truth so that there will develop within us, without our conscious effort, an everpresent horror of a lie.

If we desire to do good in the world, let us begin to love humanity, to realize, despite all the discords of life, the great natural bond of unity that makes all men brothers. Then jealousy, envy, malice, unkind words and cruel misjudgements will be eclipsed by the sunshine of love.

The greatest triumph of this century is not its marvellous progress in industry and science, its strides in education, its conquests of the uncharted regions of the world, or its increase in material comfort and wealth—the greatest triumph of the century is the sweet atmosphere of Peace that covers a nation, and the coming together of the peoples of the earth. Peace is but the breath and life of love. And love is but the angel of life that rolls away all stones of sorrow and suffering from the pathway of duty.

IV

The Supreme Charity
of the World

True charity is not typified by an almsbox.
The benevolence of a checkbook does not meet
all the wants of humanity. Giving food, clothing
and money to the poor is only the beginning,
the kindergarten class, of real charity.

Charity has higher, purer forms of manifestation. It is an instinctive reaching out for justice in life. It seeks to smooth the rough places
of living and bridge the chasms of human sin
and folly. It desires to feed the heart-hungry, to
give strength to the struggling, to be tender
with human weakness. But greatest of all, charity obeys the Divine injunction: "Judge not."

The symbol of true charity is the hand of Justice holding on high the scales of judgement. So
perfectly are they balanced that they do not dip
to one side to pronounce final judgement, because each moment adds its grain of evidence
to either side of the balance.

With this ideal before him, man, conscious of
his own weaknesses, dare not assume the Di-

vine prerogative of pronouncing final judgement on any individual. He will seek to train mind and heart to greater keeness, purity and delicacy in watching the movement of the balance in which he weighs the characters and reputations of those around him.

How often we hear people say, "I love to study character—on the streets, in cars, in a crowded room." And how little they realize that they are not studying character, but merely observing characteristics. The study of character is not a puzzle that a man may work out overnight. Character is most subtle, elusive, changing and contradictory. It is a strange mingling of habits, hopes, motives, ideals, weaknesses and memories all manifested in a thousand different phases.

There is but one quality necessary for the perfect understanding of character, and if a man has it, he may *dare to judge*. That quality is omniscience.

Most people study character as a proofreader pores over a great poem: with ears dulled to the majesty and music of the lines, with eyes darkened to the imaginative genius of the author. The proofreader is busy watching for an inverted comma, a misspacing, or a wrong letter. He has an eye trained for imperfections. Men who pride themselves on being shrewd in discovering weak points in others think they understand character, but they know only a part of character. They know merely the depths to which a man may sink. They know not the heights to which a man may rise.

We never see the target a man aims at in life. We see only the target he hits. We judge from results, and we imagine an infinity of motives that must have been in the man's mind. No human being since creation has been able to live a life so pure and noble as to exempt him from the misjudgement of those around him. It is impossible to get anything but a distorted image from a convex or a concave mirror.

If misfortune comes to a man, people are prone to say, "It is a judgement upon him." How do they know? Have they been eavesdropping at the door of Paradise? When sorrow and failure come to us, we regard them as misdirected packages that should have been delivered elsewhere. We do too much watching of our neighbor's garden, and too little weeding in our own.

Bottles have been picked up at sea thousands of miles from the point where they have been cast into the waters. They have been the sport of wind and weather, carried along by ocean currents to ports of destination undreamed of. Our flippant, careless words of judgement about someone's character, words lightly spoken, may be carried by unknown currents to bring misery and shame upon the innocent. A cruel smile, a shrug of the shoulders or a cleverly eloquent silence may ruin in a moment another's reputation, just as a single motion of the hand can destroy the delicate geometry of a spider's web—and all the efforts of the universe cannot put it back as it was.

We do not need to judge nearly so much as we think we do. This is the age of snap judgements; a habit greatly intensified by the press. Twenty-four hours after a sensational murder, it's difficult to find people who have not already formulated a judgement about the case. These people have usually read and accepted the highly-colored newspaper account and have almost discovered the murderer, tried him and sentenced him. We hear readers state their decisions with all the force and absoluteness of one who has omniscience.

If there is a time in life when the attitude of the agnostic is right, it is in the moment of judging others. It is the courage to say, "I don't know—I'm waiting on further evidence. I must hear both sides of the question. Until then, I suspend all judgement." It is this suspended judgement that is the supreme form of charity.

It is strange that most of us recognize the right of every criminal to have a fair, open trial, yet we condemn, unheard, the dear friends around us on mere circumstancial evidence. We rely on the scanty evidence of our senses, trust it implicitly, and permit it to sweep away our faith. Our hasty judgement, that a few moments of explanation would remove, thus estranges a friend. If we are this unjust to those we hold dear, what must be the cruel injustice of our judgement of others?

We know nothing of the trials, sorrows, and temptations of those around us; or of the secret struggles and worries, of perhaps a life-tragedy that may be hidden behind a smile. At times we even say to one who seems calm and smiling, "You ought to be supremely happy, you have everything a heart could wish for." And it may be that at that very moment the person is passing alone through some grief when living seems like an agony from which there is no relief. Then our misjudgements only make them feel isolated from the rest of humanity.

Let us not add to the burden of another the pain of our judgements. If we are to guard our mouths from expressing them, then we must control our minds and stop continually assessing the acts of others, even in private. By daily exercises in self-control, let us learn to turn off the process of judging as we would turn out a light. Let us eliminate pride, passion, prejudice and pettiness from our minds, and higher, purer emotions will rush in, as air seeks to fill a vacuum.

Charity is not a formula, it is an atmosphere. To cultivate charity in judging, we must learn to search out the good in others, rather than attempt to discover the hidden evils. The eye of charity requires that we see the undeveloped butterfly in the caterpillar. Let us, then, make for our watchword the phrase of supreme charity: "Judge not."

V

Worry, the Great American Disease

Worry is the most popular form of suicide. It impairs appetite, spoils digestion, disturbs sleep, irritates disposition, weakens mind, warps character, saps bodily health and stimulates disease. Worry is the real cause of death in thousands of instances where some other disease is named on the death certificate.

When a man or woman works over in dreams the problems of the day, or when the sleeping hours are spent in turning round the kaleidoscope of the day's activities, then there is worry, often due to overwork. The creator never intended a healthy mind to dream of the day's duties.

If a child's absorption in his studies keeps him from resting, or if he tosses and turns, muttering multiplication in his sleep, then that child is worrying. This is one of Nature's danger signals raised to warn parents that the burden of their child's daily tasks should be lightened and the tension of his education lessened.

When the spectre of grief, fear or sorrow obtrudes itself between the eye and the printed page; when the inner voice of irritating memory or apprehension looms up so loudly as to deaden outside voices, there is danger to the individual. We must know that we are worrying when all day, every hour, every moment, there is the dull, insistent pain of something that makes itself felt through all our other thinking. There is then, but one thing for us to do: Kill the worry.

The wise men of this century have made great discoveries in their dealings with Nature. They have learned that everything created has its uses. They can tell you what exactly are the special duties and responsibilities of every microscopic microbe that has a telescopic name. In their scientific enthusiasm they may even venture to persuade us that the *mosquito* serves some real purpose in Nature. But no man yet can truthfully say a good word about worry.

Worry is forethought gone to seed. Worry is counting possible future sorrows so that the individual may have present misery. Worry is the father of insomnia. Under the guise of helping us to bear the present, and to be ready for the future, it multiplies enemies within our own minds to sap our strength.

Worry is the dominance of the mind by a single vague, restless, unsatisfied, or fearful idea. The mental energy and force which should be concentrated on the successive duties of the day is constantly and surreptitiously abstracted and absorbed by this one fixed idea. The full strength of the unconscious working of the mind, which produces our best success and represents our finest activity, is wasted on worry.

Worry must not be confused with anxiety, although both words agree in original meaning: a "choking" or "strangling"—which refers to the throttling effect upon individual activity. Anxiety faces large issues of life seriously, calmly and with dignity. It always suggests hopeful possibilities. Worry is not one large individual sorrow, but a colony of petty, vague, insignificant, restless fears that become important only in their combination of their constancy.

When death comes, when the one we love has passed from us, and the silence and emptiness make us stare into the future, we give ourselves up for a time to the agony of isolation. This is not a petty worry we must kill before it kills us. This is the awful majesty of sorrow that mercifully benumbs us, and may later become a rebaptism and a regeneration. It is the worry *habit*, the constant magnifying of petty sorrows that eclipse the sun of happiness, against which I am making protest.

To cure worry, the individual must be his own physician; he must give his case heroic treatment, realizing, with every fiber of his being, the utter uselessness of worry. He must understand that if it was possible for him to spend a whole series of eternities in worry, it would change nothing.

If you set down a column of figures in addition, no amount of worry can change the sum total of those figures. The result can be made different only by changing the numbers as they are set down, one by one, in that column.

The one time that man cannot afford to worry is when he is facing, or imagines he is facing, a critical turn of affairs. Often this is the time when he worries most—the time when he needs one hundred percent of his mental energy to make his wisest decision quickly, to keep a clear eye on his course and a firm hand on the helm until he has weathered the storm in safety.

There are two major reasons why man should not worry, either one of which must exist in every instance. First, if he *cannot* prevent the results he fears, if he's powerless to avert a blow, he needs perfect mental concentration to meet it bravely, to lighten its force, and to sustain his strength for a new plan in the future. Second, if he *can* prevent the evil he fears, then he has no need to worry, for by doing so, he would be dissipating energy in his very hour of need.

If man does, day by day, the very best he can, he has no need to worry. No agony of worry could help him, for neither mortal nor angel can do more than his best. If we look back upon our past life, we will see how, in the marvellous working of events, our moments of greatest happiness and success have been founded upon our deepest sorrows, our most abject failures. Often our present joys would have been impossible but for some terrible affliction or loss in the past; a loss which becomes a potent force in the evolution of our character and our fortune. This should be a stimulus to us in bearing the trials and sorrows of life.

To cure one's self of worry is not an easy task. It requires clear, common sense applied to the business of life. With inalienable duties to himself, to his family and to the world, man has no right to waste his energies, or to weaken his own powers through worry.

VI

The Greatness
of Simplicity

Simplicity is the elimination of the non-essential in all things. It reduces life to its minimum of real needs and raises it to its maximum of powers. Simplicity means the survival, not of the fittest, but of the best. Morally speaking, it kills the weeds of vice and weakness so the flowers of virtue and strength have room to grow. Simplicity cuts off waste and intensifies concentration.

All great truths are simple. The essence of Christianity is in but a few words seeking to be made real through thoughts and acts. The true Christian's belief is always simpler than his church creed, and upon these vital elements he builds his life. Higher criticism never rises to the heights of his simplicity. He has no time for hair-splitting interpretations of words and phrases. Nor does he care for the anatomy of religion; he has its soul. His simple faith he lives—in thought and word and act, each day.

The minister whose sermons are made up merely of flowery rhetoric, sprigs of quotations and perfumed banalities, is, consciously or unconsciously, posing in the pulpit. His weak literary concoctions can never help a human soul or offer it strength and inspiration. If the mind and heart of the preacher were truly filled with the greatness and simplicity of religion, he would apply the realities of his faith to the vital problems of daily living. The test of a strong, simple sermon is results—not the Sunday praise of his auditors, but their bettered lives during the week. People who pray on their knees on Sunday and prey on their neighbors on Monday, need simplicity in their faith.

No character can be simple unless it is based on truth; unless it is lived in harmony with one's own conscience and ideals. Simplicity is destroyed by any attempt to live in harmony with public opinion. Public opinion is a syndicated conscience where the individual is merely a stockholder. When an individual realizes he is sole proprietor of his conscience and adjusts his life to his own ideals, he has found the royal road to simplicity.

Affectation is the confession of inferiority; it is an unnecessary proclamation that one is not living the life he pretends to live. A restless hunger for the non-essentials of life is the reason for most of the discontent in the world. It is constant striving to outshine others that kills simplicity and happiness. Simplicity is restful contempt for the non-essentials.

Nature, in all her revelations, seeks to teach

man the greatness of simplicity. Health is but the living of physical life in harmony with a few simple, clearly defined laws: simple food, simple exercise, simple precautions. But man grows tired of the simple things, yeilds to subtle temptations and then suffers. How often he listens to his palate instead of to Nature. Then he is led into intimate acquaintance with ulcers, and sits like a child at his own bounteous table, forced to limit his eating to the simple food he once scorned.

There is a tonic strength in the hour of sorrow and affliction, in escaping from the world and getting back to the simple duties and interests we have slighted and forgotten. Our world grows smaller, but it grows dearer and greater. Simple things have a new charm for us, and we suddenly realize that we have been renouncing all that is best in pursuit of phantoms.

Simplicity is the characteristic most difficult to simulate. The signature that is hardest to imitate is the one that is most simple, most individual. The banknote most difficult to counterfeit successfully is the one that contains the fewest lines and has the least intricate detail So simple it is, that any departure from the normal is instantly apparent. So it is also with man's mind and morals.

Simplicity in act is the outward expression of simplicity in thought. Great men are those who are quiet, modest, unassuming. They are often made gentle, calm and simple by the discipline of their responsibility. They have no room in their minds for the pettiness of personal vanity or affectation.

Life grows wondrously beautiful when we look at it as simple, when we can brush aside trivial cares, sorrows, worries and failures, and say: "They don't count. They're not the real things of life, only interruptions. Within my individuality, there is something that makes all these gnats of trouble seem too trifling for me to allow them dominion over me." Simplicity is a mental soil where selfishness, deceit, treachery and low ambition cannot grow.

The man whose character is simple has no consciousness of intrigue and corruption about him. He is deaf to the hints and whispers of wrong that a suspicious nature would suspect even before they exist. He scorns the idea of meeting intrigue with intrigue or holding power by bribery. Nothing great can ever enter into the mind of a man of simplicity and remain just a theory. When he perceives truth, he begins to live it. Simplicity in a character is like the needle of a compass: it knows only one point—its North, its ideal.

Let us seek to cultivate this simplicity in all aspects of our lives. The first step toward simplicity is simplifying. The beginning of mental or moral progress or reform is always renunciation or sacrifice. It is rejection, surrender or destruction of habits or attitude that have kept us from higher things. Reform your diet and you simplify it; reform your morals and you begin to cut off immoral behavior.

The secret of all true greatness is simplicity. Make simplicity the keynote of your life and you will be great, no matter if your life be humble and your influence seem but little. Simple habits, simple manners, simple needs, simple words, simple faiths; all are the pure manifestations of a great mind and heart.

Simplicity means the light of fullest knowledge. It means that the individual has seen the folly and the nothingness of those things which make up the sum of the lives of others. He has lived *down* what others are blindly seeking to live *up* to. Simplicity is the secret of greatness in the life of every human being.

VII

Living Life Over Again

During a terrific storm a few years ago a ship was driven far off her course and helpless and disabled, was carried into a strange bay. The water supply gave out, and the crew suffered the agony of thirst, yet dared not drink of the salt water in which their vessel floated. Finally, in a last act of desperation, they lowered a bucket over the ship's side and quaffed what they thought was sea water. But to their amazement and joy the water was fresh. They were in a freshwater arm of the sea, and they did not know it They had simply to reach down and accept the new life-giving strength for which they had prayed.

Man today, heart-weary with the sorrow, sin and failure of his past life, feels that he could live a better life if he could only live it over again; if he could only start afresh with his present knowledge and experience. He looks back with regretful memory to the golden days of youth and sadly mourns his wasted chances. He then turns hopefully to the thought of a new future, as he stands between the two ends of life. Blindly desiring the chance to live a new existence according to his bettered condition for living it, he does not realize that the new life is all around him. Like the storm-driven sailors, he has but to reach out and take it. Every day is a new existence, every sunrise but a new birth for himself and the world. Each morning is the beginning of a new life, a new, great chance to put to higher uses the results of his past living.

The man who looks back upon his past life and says, "I have nothing to regret," has lived in vain. The life without regret is the life without gain. Regret is the light of fuller wisdom from our past, illuminating the future. It means that we are wiser today than we were yesterday. This new wisdom means new responsibility, new privileges and a chance for a better life. But if regret remains merely "regret," it is useless. It must become the inspiration and source of strength to realize new possibilities. Even omnipotence could not change the past. But each man, to a degree far beyond his knowing, holds his future in his own hands.

If man were sincere in his longing to live life over, he would get more help from his failures. If he realizes his wasted opportunities, let him not waste other hours in useless regret, but seek to forget his folly and keep before him only the lessons of it. His past extravagance of time should lead him to minimize his loss by a marvellous economy of present moments. If his whole life is darkened by the memory of a cruel wrong he has done another, and direct amends are impossible to the injured one, let him make the world the beneficiary of his restitution. Let his regret and sorrow be manifested in words of kindness, in acts of love given to all with whom he comes in contact. If he regrets war he has made against another individual, let him place the entire world on his pension list. If a man make a certain mistake once, the only way he can properly express his repentance is not to make a similar mistake again. Josh Billings once said, "A man who is bitten twice by the same dog is better adapted to that business than any other."

There are many people in this world who want to live life over because they take such pride in their past. They resemble the beggars in the street who tell you they "have seen better days." It is not what man *was* that shows character; it is what he progressively *is*. Trying to obtain a present record on a dead past is like covering up your mediocrity with your ancestry. We look for the fruit in the branches of the family tree, not in the roots. Let man think less of his own ancestors and more of those he is preparing for his posterity; less of his past virtue, and more of the good he can accomplish in the future.

When a man pleads for a chance to live life over, he is expressing a lack of knowledge, unworthy even of a coward. We know the laws of health, yet we ignore them every day. We know what is the proper food for us, individually, yet we gratify our appetites and trust to our cleverness to square the account with Nature somehow. We know that success is a matter of simple, clearly defined laws, of the development of mental essentials, of tireless energy and concentration, of a constant payment of price. We know all this, and yet we do not live up to our knowledge. Instead, we blame Fate.

Parents often counsel their children against certain things and then do those very things themselves, foolishly hoping that the children will believe their ears and not their eyes. Years of teaching a child to be honest and truthful may be nullified in an instant by a parent's lying to a ticket-seller about the child's age to save half-fare. That can be an exceedingly expensive ticket for both the child and the parent. It may be part of the spirit of the times to believe it is no sin to cheat an institution, but it is unwise to give the child so striking an example at an age when he cannot discern the falsity of it.

Man's only excuse for a chance to live life again is that he has gained in wisdom and experience. If he is really in earnest then he can start life afresh, leaving to the past all his mistakes, sin, sorrow, misery and folly, and live the new life that comes to him day by day. Let him credit himself with the knowledge he has gained from his past failures and charge himself with the responsibilities that come from the possession of his new wisdom. Let him criticize others less and himself more. Let him be honest at all times as he starts out bravely in his new life.

What we need is more day-to-day living; starting in the morning with fresh, clear ideals for that day, and seeking to live each hour as if it were all the time left to us. This has in it no element of disregard for the future, because each day is set in harmony with that future. It is like the sea captain pointing his vessel toward its port of destination and day by day keeping her sailing toward it. This view of living kills morbid regret of the past and morbid worry about the future.

Life is worth living if it is lived in a way that is worth living. At each New Year it is common to make new resolutions, but in the life of the individual, each day is the beginning of a New Year, if he will only make it so. A mere date on the calendar is no more a divider of time that a particular grain of sand divides the desert.

Let us not make heroic resolutions so far beyond our strength that the resolution becomes a dead memory within a week. But let us promise ourselves that each day will be the new beginning of a better life, not only for ourselves, but for those close to us and the world as well.

VIII

Syndicating Our Sorrows

The most selfish man in the world is the one who is most unselfish with his sorrows. He does not leave a single misery untold to you, or unsuffered by you. He gives you all of them. The world becomes to him a dumping ground of his private cares, worries and trials.

Life is a great, serious problem for the individual. All our greatest joys and our deepest sorrows come to us—alone. We must go into our Gethsemane—alone. Alone, we must battle against the mighty weaknesses within us. And we must live our own lives—and die—alone. If each one of us has this great problem of life to solve for himself, if each of us has his own cares, responsibilities, failures, doubts, fears, we surely are playing a coward's part when we syndicate our sorrows.

We should seek to make life brighter for others. Through our courage in bearing our own sorrows, we can seek to hearten others in their times of trial. Seeking to forget our failures and remembering only the new wisdom they've brought us, we can live down our griefs by counting the joys and privileges still left to us. We have no right to retail our sorrow and unhappiness throughout the community.

Autobiography constitutes a large part of the conversation of some people. It is not really conversation, but more like uninterrupted monologue. These people study their individual lives with a microscope, and then they throw an enlarged view of their miseries on a screen and lecture on them, as a biologist discourses on the microbes in a drop of water. They tell you that "they did not sleep a wink all night; they heard the clock strike every quarter of an hour." Now, there is no real cause for boasting of insomnia. Even though it only comes to wide-awake people, it requires no peculiar talent.

If you ask such a man how he is feeling, he will trace the whole genealogy of his present condition down from the time he had influenza four years ago. You hoped for a word; he gives you a treatise. You asked for a sentence; he delivers an encyclopedia. Such a person is syndicating his sorrows.

The woman who makes her trials and troubles with her family the subjects of conversation, is syndicating her sorrows as well. If she has a dear, little child who recites, "Curfew Shall Not Ring Tonight," is it not wiser for the mother to bear it in discreet silence rather than to syndicate her difficulty?

The business man who lets his indigestion get

into his disposition, and who makes everyone around him suffer because of it, is syndicating his ill health. We have no right to make others the victims of our moods. If illness makes us cross and irritable, makes us unjust to employees and co-workers, let us quarantine ourselves so that we do not spread the contagion. Let us force ourselves to keep temper from showing in our voices. If we feel we *must* have indigestion, let us keep it from getting to our heads.

Most people sympathize too much with themselves. They take themselves as a single sentence isolated from the great text of life; studying themselves as if separated from the rest of humanity, instead of being vitally connected with their fellow men. Some people surrender to sorrow like others give way to dissipation. Most individuals, when looking back upon their past feelings, believe that few others in life have suffered such trials as have come to them. There is a vain pride of sorrow as well as of beauty.

When death comes into the circle of loved ones that make up our world, all life becomes darkened. We seem to have no reason for existing, no incentive, no hope. The love that made effort and struggle bearable for us, is gone. Life becomes but a memory; a past with no future.

Then in the divine mystery of Nature's processes, under the soothing touch of Time, as days melt into weeks, we begin to open our eyes gently to the world around us and the noise and tumult of life jars us less and less. We have become emotionally convalescent. As the days go on, in our deep love and loyalty, we protest often against our gradual return to the spirit and atmosphere of the days of the past. We feel a subtle new pain, as if we are being disloyal to the dead one, faithless to our love. Nature turns aside our protesting hands, and says to us, "There is no disloyalty in permitting your wounds to hurt less, to heal gradually." There are some natures all-absorbed in a mighty love, where no healing is possible, but these are rare souls in life.

Bitter though our anguish is, we have no right to syndicate our sorrow. We have no right to cast a gloom over happy natures by our heavy burden of grief, by serving the term prescribed by Society for wearing the livery of mourning, as if real sorrow is a uniform. We have no right to syndicate our grief by parading our personal sorrow to others in their happy moments.

If life has not gone well with us, if fortune has left us disconsolate, if love has grown cold, let us not radiate such an atmosphere to those around us. Let us not take strangers through the catacombs of our lives, showing them the bones of the dead past. Neither let us pass our cup of sorrow to others, but if we must drink it, let us take it as Socrates did his hemlock: grandly, heroically and without complaint.

If your life has led you to doubt the existence of honor in man, or the virtue in woman; if you feel that religion is a pretense, that spirituality is a sham, and death the entrance to nothingness; if you have absorbed all the poisonous philosophies of the world's pessimists, and committed the folly of believing much of it, don't syndicate it. If your fellow man is clinging to one frail spar, the last remnant of a noble, shipwrecked faith in God and humanity, let him keep it. Do not loosen his fingers from his hope and tell him it is a delusion. How do you know it is so?

You may have one person in the world to whom you dare show, in confidence and faith, your thoughts, hopes and sorrows. Wisely, you dare not trust such cares to the world. Keeping your trials and sorrows as close to you as you can till you have mastered them, you will not weaken others by syndicating your miseries.

IX

The Revelations
of Reserve Power

Every individual is a marvel of unknown and unrealized possibilities. Nine-tenths of an iceberg is always below water. Nine-tenths of the possibilities of good and evil in an individual are hidden from his sight.

Burns' prayer, that we might "see ourselves as others see us," speaks only to man's vanity. What others see him as being, is often not what a man is. We should pray to see ourselves as we *are*. But no man could face the radiant revelation of the latent powers and forces within him, underlying the weak, narrow life he is living. He would fall blinded and prostrate, as Moses did before the burning bush. Man is not a mechanical box wound up by the Creator and set to play a fixed number of prescribed tunes. He is a human harp, with infinite possibilities for creating unrealized music.

The untold revelations of Nature are in her Reserve Power, her method of meeting emergencies. Nature is wise and economic. Nature saves energy and effort, and gives only what is absolutely necessary for life and development under any given condition. When new needs arise, Nature always meets them through her Reserve Power.

In animal life, Nature reveals this in a million phases. Animals placed in the darkness of the Mammoth Cave gradually have their sense of sight weakened and their senses of smell, touch and hearing intensified. Nature watches over all animals, making their colors harmonize with their surroundings to protect them from their enemies. Those arctic animals which in summer inhabit regions free from snow, turn white when the winter comes. In the desert, the animals have more or less the color of the sand and rocks among which they live. In tropical forests, parrots are usually green, as are many of the other inhabitants like lizards and insects. As the habits of the animals change, from generation to generation, so do their colors. Nature, through her Reserve Power, always meets the new needs of animals with new strength, giving them new harmony with their new conditions.

About forty-five years ago, three pairs of enterprising rabbits were introduced into Australia. Today, the increase of these six immigrants may be counted in the millions. They became a national pest and fortunes have been spent to exterminate them. Wire fences many feet high and hundreds of miles long have been built to keep them from invading croplands. But the rabbits have outwitted man. They have developed over the years, a claw which enables them to climb a fence as well as burrow beneath it in order to reach the fields which mean food and life to them. Nature's Reserve Power has given these rabbits latent possibilities in their struggle to survive, because they did not tamely accept their condition.

Nature is a great believer in "double engines." Man is equipped with many parts of his body in duplicate—eyes, ears, lungs, arms, legs, If one is weakened, its mate, through Reserve Power, is stimulated to do enough for both. Even when the organ itself is not duplicated, as in the nose, there is a division of parts so that there is constant reserve. Nature, for still further protection, has for every part of the human body, an understudy to be ready in a crisis: as the sense of touch for the blind.

Nature, thus watching so tenderly over the physical needs of man, is equally provident in storing for him a mental and moral Reserve Power. Man may fail in a dozen different lines of activity and then succeed brilliantly in an area wherein he was unconscious of any ability at all. We must never rest with what we *are,* saying, "There is no use for me to try to be great, I am not even mediocre." We must listen to the law of Reserve Power which says: "There is one charm by which you can transmute the dull dross of your present condition into the shining gold of strength and power. That charm is simply doing your best always; always daring more.

The full measure of your final attainment can never be told in advance. Rely upon me to help you with new revelations in new emergencies."

Never be cast down because your power seems trifling, your progress slow. The world's greatest men were failures in some line, failures many times before failure was crowned with success.

There is, in the mythology of the Norseman, a belief that the strength of an enemy we have killed enters into us. This is true in character. As we conquer a passion, a thought, a feeling, as we rise above some impulse, the strength of that victory, trifling though it may be, is stored by Nature as a Reserve Power to come to us in the hour of our need.

Were we to place before almost any individual the full chart of his future—his trials, sorrows, failures, afflictions, loss, sickness and loneliness—and ask him if he could bear it, he would say, "No! I could not bear all that and live." But he *can* and he *does*. The hopes upon which he has staked his future turn to mist as he nears them; friends whom he has trusted betray him; the world grows cold to him as the child whose smile is the light of his life dishonors his name; death takes from him the love of his dearest ones—yet Reserve Power has been giving him new strength to carry on after each crisis.

If we are conscious of any weakness and have the desire to conquer it, we can force ourselves into positions where we *must* act in a way to strengthen ourselves through that weakness. Reserve Power is like the manna given to the children of Israel, only enough was given them to keep them for one day. Each successive day had its new supply of strength. There is in the Leaning Tower of Pisa a spiral staircase so steep in its ascent that only one step at a time is revealed as one is climbing it. But as each step is taken, the next is made visible, and so it goes, step by step, to the very top.

In the divine economy of the universe, Reserve Power is a gradual and constant revelation of strength within us to meet each new need. And no matter what is our walk of life, what are our needs, we should feel that we have within us infinite, untried strengths and possibilities—that if we believe and do our best, the Angel of Reserve Power will walk by our side, dividing even the waters of our trials and sorrows, so we may walk in safety.

AS A MAN THINKETH

by

James Allen

About the Author

Very little is known about James Allen (1864–1912). He is often confused with the American writer of the same name who lived in Kentucky during the nineteenth century. Research proves, however, that James Allen, the Kentuckian, was not the author of *As a Man Thinketh*.

Along with the dates of Allen's birth and decease, we do know that he wrote *As a Man Thinketh* in Ilfracombe, England, and that his message went out from there to encompass the world for generations. His "little volume", as he calls it, has been translated into five major languages, inspiring millions of readers to recognize that man's visions can become reality, simply through the power of thought.

Foreward

This little volume (the result of meditation and experience) is not intended as an exhaustive treatise on the much-written-upon subject of the power of thought. It is suggestive rather than explanatory, its object being to stimulate men and women to the discovery and perception of the truth that "They themselves are makers of themselves" by virtue of the thoughts which they choose and encourage; that mind is the master-weaver, both of the inner garment of character and the outer garment of circumstance, and that, as they may have hitherto woven in ignorance and pain, they may now weave in enlightenment and happiness.

JAMES ALLEN

Thought and Character

The aphorism, "As a man thinketh in his heart so is he," not only embraces the whole of a man's being, but is so comprehensive as to reach out to every condition and circumstance of his life. A man is literally *what he thinks,* his character being the complete sum of all his thoughts.

As the plant springs from, and could not be without, the seed, so every act of a man springs from the hidden seeds of thought, and could not have appeared without them. This applies equally to those acts called "spontaneous" and "unpremeditated" as to those which are deliberately executed.

Act is the blossom of thought, and joy and suffering are its fruits; thus does a man garner in the sweet and bitter fruitage of his own husbandry.

Thought in the mind hath made us.
What we are by thought was wrought and
  built.
If a man's mind hath evil thoughts,

Pain comes on him as comes the wheel the ox
  behind,
If one endure in purity of thought,
Joy follows him as his own shadow—sure.

Man is a growth by law, and not a creation
by artifice, and cause and effect is as absolute
and undeviating in the hidden realm of thought
as in the world of visible and material things.
A noble and Godlike character is not a thing of
favor or chance, but is the natural result of continued effort in right thinking, the effect of long-
cherished association with Godlike thoughts. An
ignoble and bestial character, by the same process, is the result of the continued harboring of
groveling thoughts.

Man is made or unmade by himself; in the
armory of thought he forges the weapons by
which he destroys himself; he also fashions the
tools with which he builds for himself heavenly
mansions of joy and strength and peace. By the
right choice and true application of thought, man
ascends to the Divine Perfection. By the abuse
and wrong application of thought, he descends
below the level of the beast. Between these two
extremes are all the grades of character, and
man is their maker and master.

Of all the beautiful truths pertaining to the
soul which have been restored and brought to
light in this age, none is more gladdening or
fruitful of divine promise and confidence than
this—that man is the master of thought, the

molder of character, and the maker and shaper of condition, environment, and destiny. As a being of Power, Intelligence, and Love, and the lord of his own thoughts, man holds the key to every situation, and contains within himself that transforming and regenerative agency by which he may make himself what he wills.

Man is always the master, even in his weakest and most abandoned state; but in his weakness and degradation he is the foolish master who misgoverns his household. When he begins to reflect upon his condition, and to search diligently for the Law upon which his being is established, he then becomes the wise master, directing his energies with intelligence, and fashioning his thoughts to fruitful issues. Such is the *conscious* master, and man can only thus become by discovering *within himself* the laws of thought; which discovery is totally a matter of application, self-analysis, and experience.

Only by much searching and mining are gold and diamonds obtained, and man can find every truth connected with his being if he will dig deep into the mine of his soul. That he is the maker of his character, the molder of his life, and the builder of his destiny, he may unerringly prove, if he will watch, control, and alter his thoughts, tracing their effects upon himself, upon others, and upon his life and circumstances, linking cause and effect by patient practice and investigation, and utilizing his every experience, even to the most trivial, everyday occurrence, as a means of obtaining that knowledge of himself which is Understanding, Wisdom, Power. In this direction, as in no other, is the law absolute that "He that seeketh findeth; and to him that knocketh it shall be opened; "for only by patience, practice, and ceaseless importunity can a man enter the Door of the Temple of Knowledge.

Effect of Thought on Circumstances

A man's mind may be likened to a garden, which may be intelligently cultivated or allowed to run wild; but whether cultivated or neglected, it must, and will, *bring forth*. If no useful seeds are *put* into it, then an abundance of useless weed-seeds will *fall* therein, and will continue to produce their kind.

Just as a gardener cultivates his plot, keeping it free from weeds, and growing the flowers and fruits which he requires, so may a man tend the garden of his mind, weeding out all the wrong, useless, and impure thoughts, and cultivating toward perfection the flowers and fruits of right, useful, and pure thoughts. By pursuing this process, a man sooner or later discovers that he is the master-gardener of his soul, the director of his life. He also reveals, within himself, the laws of thought, and understands with ever-increasing accuracy, how the thought-forces and mind-elements operate in the shaping of his character, circumstances, and destiny.

Thought and character are one, and as character can only manifest and discover itself through environment and circumstance, the outer conditions of a person's life will always be found to be harmoniously related to his inner state. This does not mean that a man's circumstances at any given time are an indication of his *entire* character, but that those circumstances are so intimately connected with some vital thought-element within himself that, for the time being, they are indispensable to his development.

Every man is where he is by the law of his being. The thoughts which he has built into his character have brought him there, and in the arrangement of his life there is no element of chance, but all is the result of a law which cannot err. This is just as true of those who feel "out of harmony" with their surroundings as of those who are contented with them.

As a progressive and evolving being, man is where he is so that he may learn that he may grow; and as he learns the spiritual lesson which any circumstance contains for him, it passes away and gives place to other circumstances.

Man is buffeted by circumstances so long as he believes himself to be the creature of outside conditions. Yet, when he realizes that he is a creative power, and that he may command the hidden soil and seeds of his being out of which circumstances grow, he then becomes the rightful master of himself.

That circumstances *grow* out of thought, every

man knows who has for any length of time practiced self-control and self-purification, for he will have noticed that the alteration in his circumstances has been in exact ratio with his altered mental condition. So true is this that when a man earnestly applies himself to remedy the defects in his character, and makes swift and marked progress, he passes rapidly through a succession of vicissitudes.

The soul attracts that which it secretly harbors, that which it loves, and also that which it fears. It reaches the height of its cherished aspirations; it falls to the level of its unchastened desires, and circumstances are the means by which the soul receives its own.

Every thought-seed sown or allowed to fall into the mind, and to take root there, produces its own, blossoming sooner or later into act, and bearing its own fruitage of opportunity and circumstance. Good thoughts bear good fruit, bad thoughts bad fruit.

The outer world of circumstance shapes itself to the inner world of thought, and both pleasant and unpleasant external conditions are factors which make for the ultimate good of the individual. As the reaper of his own harvest, man learns both by suffering and bliss.

Following the inmost desires, aspirations, thoughts, by which he allows himself to be dominated (pursuing the will-o'-the-wisps of impure imagining or steadfastly walking the highway of strong and high endeavor), a man at last arrives at their fruition and fulfillment in the outer condition of his life.

The laws of growth and adjustment everywhere obtain. A man does not come to the almshouse or the jail by the tyranny of fate or circumstance, but by the pathway of groveling thoughts and base desires. Nor does a pure-minded man fall suddenly into crime by stress of any mere external force. The criminal thought had long been secretly fostered in the heart, and the hour of opportunity revealed its gathered power. Circumstance does not make the man; it reveals him to himself. No such conditions can exist as descending into vise and its attendant sufferings apart from vicious inclinations; or ascending into virtue and its pure happiness without the continued cultivation of virtuous aspirations. Man, therefore, as the lord and master of thought, is the maker of himself, the shaper and author of environment. Even at birth the soul comes to its own, and through every step of its earthly pilgrimage it attracts those combinations of conditions which reveal itself, which are the reflections of its own purity and impurity, its strength and weakness.

Men do not attract that which they *want,* but that which they *are.* Their whims, fancies, and ambitions are thwarted at every step, but their inmost thoughts and desires are fed with their own food, be it foul or clean. The "divinity that shapes our ends" is in ourselves; it is our very self. Man is manacled only by himself. Thought and action are the jailers of Fate—they imprison, being base; they are also the angels of Freedom—they liberate, being noble.

Not what he wishes and prays for does a man get, but what he justly earns. His wishes and prayers are only gratified and answered when they harmonize with his thoughts and actions.

In the light of this truth, what, then, is the meaning of "fighting against circumstances?" It means that a man is continually revolting against an *effect* without, while all the time he is nourishing and preserving its *cause* in his heart.

That cause may take the form of a conscious vice or an unconscious weakness; but whatever it is, it stubbornly retards the efforts of its possessor, and thus calls aloud for remedy.

Men are anxious to improve their circumstances, but are unwilling to improve themselves; they therefore remain bound. The man who does not shrink from self-crucifixion can never fail to accomplish the object upon which his heart is set. This is as true of earthly as of heavenly things. Even the man whose sole object is to acquire wealth must be prepared to make great personal sacrifices before he can accomplish his object; and how much more so, he who would realize a strong and well-poised life?

Here is a man who is wretchedly poor. He is extremely anxious that his surroundings and home comforts should improve, yet all the time he shirks his work, and considers he is justified in trying to deceive his employer on the ground of the insufficiency of his wages. Such a man does not understand the simplest rudiments of those principles which are the basis of true prosperity, and is not only totally unfitted to rise out of his wretchedness, but is actually attracting to himself a still deeper wretchedness by dwelling in, and acting out, indolent, deceptive, and unmanly thoughts.

Here is a rich man who is the victim of a painful and persistent disease as the result of gluttony. He is willing to give large sums of money to get rid of it, but he will not sacrifice his gluttonous desires. He wants to gratify his taste for rich and unnatural viands and have his health as well. Such a man is totally unfit to have health, because he has not yet learned the first principles of a healthy life.

Here is an employer of labor who adopts crooked measures to avoid paying the regulation wage, and, in the hope of making larger profits, reduces the wages of his workers. Such a man is altogether unfitted for prosperity, and when he finds himself bankrupt, both as regards reputation and riches, he blames circumstances, not knowing that he is the sole author of his condition.

I have introduced these three cases merely as illustrative of the truth that man is the causer (though nearly always unconsciously) of his circumstances, and that, whilst aiming at a good end, he is continually frustrating its accomplishment by encouraging thoughts and desires which cannot possibly harmonize with that end. Such cases could be multiplied and varied almost indefinitely, but this is not necessary, as the reader can, if he so resolves, trace the action of the laws of thought in his own mind and life, and until this is done, mere external facts cannot serve as a ground of reasoning.

Circumstances, however, are so complicated, thought so deeply rooted, and the conditions of happiness vary so vastly with individuals, that a man's *entire* soul-condition (although it may be known to himself) cannot be judged by another from the external aspect of his life alone. A man may be honest in certain directions, yet suffer privations; a man may be dishonest in certain directions, yet acquire wealth; but the conclusion usually formed that the one man fails *because of his particular honesty,* and that the other prospers *because of his particular dishonesty,* is the result of a superficial judgement, which assumes that the dishonest man is almost totally corrupt, and the honest man almost entirely virtuous. In the light of a deeper knowledge and wider experience, such judgement is found to be erroneous. The dishonest man may have some admirable virtues which the other does not possess; and the honest man obnoxious vices which are absent in the other. The honest man reaps the good results of his honest thoughts and acts; he also brings upon himself the suffering which his vices produce. Th dishonest man likewise garners his own suffering and happiness.

It is pleasing to human vanity to believe that one suffers because of one's virtue; but not until a man has extirpated every sickly, bitter, and impure thought from his mind, and washed every sinful stain from his soul, can he be in a position to know and declare that his sufferings are the result of his good, and not of his bad qualities. On the way to, yet long before he has reached, that supreme perfection, he will have found, working in his mind and life, the Great Law which is absolutely just, and which cannot, therefore, give good for evil, evil for good. Possessed of such knowledge, he will then know, looking back upon his past ignorance and blindness, that his life is, and always was, justly ordered, and that all his past experiences, good and bad, were the equitable outworking of his evolving, yet unevolved self.

Good thoughts and actions can never produce bad results; bad thoughts and actions can never produce good results. This is but saying that nothing can come from corn but corn, nothing from nettles but nettles. Men understand this law in the natural world and work with it; but few understand it in the mental and moral world (though its operation there is just as simple and undeviating), and they therefore, do not cooperate with it.

Suffering is *always* the effect of wrong thought

in some direction. It is an indication that the individual is out of harmony with himself, with the Law of his being. The sole and supreme use of suffering is to purify, to burn out all that is useless and impure. Suffering ceases for him who is pure. There could be no object in burning gold after the dross had been removed, and a perfectly pure and enlightened being could not suffer.

The circumstances which a man encounters with suffering are the result of his own mental disharmony. The circumstances which a man encounters with blessedness are the result of his own mental harmony. Blessedness, not material possessions, is the measure of right thought; wretchedness, not a lack of material possessions, is the measure of wrong thought. A man may be cursed and rich; he may be blessed and poor. Blessedness and riches are only joined together when the riches are rightly and wisely used; and the poor man only descends into wretchedness when he regards his lot as a burden unjustly imposed.

Indigence and indulgence are the two extremes of wretchedness. They are both equally unnatural and the result of mental disorder. A man is not rightly conditioned until he is a happy, healthy, and prosperous being; and happiness, health, and prosperity are the result of a harmonious adjustment of the inner with the outer, of the man with his surroundings.

A man only begins to be a man when he ceases to whine and revile, and commences to search for the hidden justice which regulates his life. And as he adapts his mind to that regulating factor, he ceases to accuse others as the cause of his condition, and he builds himself up in strong and noble thoughts; ceases to kick against circumstances, but begins to *use* them as aids to his more rapid progress, and as a means of discovering the hidden powers and possibilities within himself.

Law, not confusion, is the dominating principle in the universe. Justice, not injustice, is the soul and substance of life. Righteousness, not corruption, is the molding and moving force in the spiritual government of the world. This being so, man has but to right himself to find that the universe is right; and during the process of putting himself right, he will find that as he alters his thoughts towards things and other people, things and other people will alter towards him.

The proof of this truth is in every person, and it therefore admits of easy investigation by systematic introspection and self-analysis. Let a man radically alter his thoughts, and he will be astonished at the rapid transformation it will effect in the material conditions of his life. Men imagine that thought can be kept secret, but it cannot; it rapidly crystallizes into habit, and habit solidifies into circumstance. Bestial thoughts crystallize into habits of drunkeness and sensuality, which solidify into circumstances of destitution and disease. Impure thoughts of every kind crystallize into enervating and confusing habits, which solidify into distracting and adverse circumstances. Thoughts of fear, doubt, and indecision crystallize into weak, unmanly, and irresolute habits which solidify into circumstances of failure, indigence, and slavish dependence. Lazy thoughts crystallize into habits of uncleanliness and dishonesty, which solidify into circumstances of foulness and beggary. Hateful and condemnatory thoughts crystallize into habits of accusations and violence, which solidify into circumstances of injury and persecution. Selfish thoughts of all kinds crystallize into habits of self-seeking which solidify into circumstances more or less distressing. On the other hand, beautiful thoughts of all kinds crystallize into habits of grace and kindliness, which solidify into genial and sunny circumstances. Pure thoughts crystallize into habits of temperance and self-control, which solidify into circumstances of repose and peace. Thoughts of courage, self-reliance and decision crystallize into manly habits, which solidify into circumstances of success, plenty, and freedom. Energetic thoughts crystallize into habits of cleanliness and industry, which solidify into circumstances of pleasantness. Kind and forgiving thoughts crystallize into habits of gentleness, which solidify into protective and preservative circumstances. Loving and unselfish thoughts crystallize into habits of self-forgetfullness for others, which solidify into circumstances of sure and abiding prosperity and true riches.

A particular train of thought persisted in, be it good or bad, cannot fail to produce its results on the character and circumstances. A man cannot *directly* choose his circumstances, but he can choose his thoughts, and so indirectly, yet surely, shape his circumstances.

Nature helps every man to the gratification of the thoughts which he most encourages, and opportunities are presented which will most speedily bring to the surface both the good and evil thoughts. Let a man cease from his sinful thoughts, and all the world will soften towards him, and be ready to help him. Let him put away his weak and sickly thoughts, and lo! opportunities will spring up on every hand to aid his strong resolves. Let him encourage good thoughts, and no hard fate shall bind him down to wretchedness and shame. The world is your kaleidoscope, and the varying combinations of colors which at every succeeding moment it presents to you are the exquisitely adjusted pictures of your evermoving thoughts.

You will be what you will be;
Let failure find its false content
In that poor word, "environment,"
But spirit scorns it, and is free.

It masters time, it conquers space;
It cows that boastful trickster, Chance,

And bids the tyrant Circumstance
Uncrown, and fill a servant's place.

The human Will, that force unseen,
The offspring of a deathless Soul,
Can hew a way to any goal,
Though walls of granite intervene.

Be not impatient in delay,
But wait as one who understands;
When spirit rises and commands,
The gods are ready to obey.

The Effect of Thought
on Health and Body

The body is the servant of the mind. It obeys the operations of the mind, whether they be deliberately chosen or automatically expressed. At the bidding of unlawful thoughts the body sinks rapidly into disease and decay. At the command of glad and beautiful thoughts it becomes clothed with youthfulness and beauty.

Disease and health, like circumstances, are rooted in thought. Sickly thoughts will express themselves through a sickly body. Thoughts of fear have been known to kill a man as speedily as a bullet, and they are continually killing thousands of people just as surely though less rapidly. The people who live in fear of disease are the people who get it. Anxiety quickly demoralizes the whole body, and lays it open to the creature of disease; while impure thoughts, even if not physically indulged, will soon shatter the nervous system.

Strong, pure and happy thoughts build up the body in vigor and grace. The body is a delicate and plastic instrument, which responds readily to the thoughts by which it is impressed, and habits of thought will produce their own effects, good or bad, upon it.

Men will continue to have impure and poisoned blood so long as they propagate unclean thoughts. Out of a clean heart comes a clean life and a clean body. Out of a defiled mind proceeds a defiled life and a corrupt body. Thought is the fount of action, life and manifestations; make the fountain pure, and all will be pure.

Change of diet will not help a man who will not change his thoughts. When a man makes his thoughts pure, he no longer desires impure food.

Clean thoughts make clean habits. The so-called saint who does not wash his body is not a saint. He who has strengthened and purified his thoughts does not need to consider the malevolent microbe.

If you would perfect your body, guard your mind. If you would renew your body, beautify your mind. Thoughts of malice, envy, disappointment, despondency, rob the body of its health and grace.. A sour face does not come by chance; it is made by sour thoughts.

Wrinkles that mar are drawn by folly, passion, pride. I know a woman of ninety-six who has the bright, innocent face of a girl. I know a man well under middle age whose face is drawn into inharmonious contours. The one is the result of a sweet and sunny disposition; the other is the outcome of passion and discontent.

As you cannot have a sweet and wholesome abode unless you admit the air and sunshine freely into your rooms, so a strong body and a bright, happy, or serene countenance can only result from the free admittance into the mind of thoughts of joy and good will and serenity.

On the faces of the aged there are wrinkles made by sympathy; others by strong and pure thought; and others are carved by passion. Who cannot distinguish them? With those who have lived righteously, age is calm, peaceful, and softly mellowed, like the setting sun. I have recently seen a philosopher on his deathbed; he was not old except in years. He died as sweetly and peacefully as he had lived.

There is no physician like cheerful thought for dissipating the ills of the body. There is no comforter to compare with good will for dispersing the shadows of grief and sorrow. To live continually in thoughts of ill will, cynicism, suspicion, and envy, is to be confined to a self-made prison. But to think well of all, to be cheerful with all, to patiently learn to find the good in all—such unselfish thoughts are the very portals of heaven; and to dwell day by day in thoughts of peace toward every creature will bring abounding peace to their possessor.

Thought and Purpose

Until thought is linked with purpose there is no intelligent accomplishment. With the majority the barque of thought is allowed to drift upon the ocean of life. Aimlessness is a vice, and such drifting must not continue for him who would steer clear of catastrophe and destruction.

They who have no central purpose in life fall easy prey to petty worries, fears, troubles, and self-pitying, all of which lead, just as surely as deliberately planned sins (though by a different route), to failure, unhappiness, and loss; for weakness cannot persist in a power-evolving universe.

A man should conceive of a legitimate purpose in his heart, and set out to accomplish it. He should make this purpose the centralizing point of his thoughts. It may take the form of a spiritual ideal, or it may be a worldly object, according to his nature at the time; but whichever it is, he should steadily focus his thought-forces upon the object which he has set before him. He should make this purpose his supreme duty, and should devote himself to its attainment, not allowing his thoughts to wander away into ephemeral fancies, longings, and imaginings. This is the royal road to self-control and true concentration of thought. Even if he fails again and again to accomplish his purpose (as he necessarily must until weakness is overcome), the *strength of character gained* will be the measure of his true success, and this will form a new starting point for future power and triumph.

Those who are not prepared for the apprehension of a *great* purpose should fix their thoughts upon the faultless performance of their duty, no matter how insignificant their task may appear. Only in this way can the thoughts be gathered and focused, and resolution and energy be developed, which being done, there is nothing which may not be accomplished.

The weakest soul, knowing its own weakness, and believing this truth—that *strength can only be developed by effort and practice,* will, thus believing, at once begin to exert itself, and, adding effort to effort, patience to patience, and strength to strength, will never cease to develop, and will at last grow divinely strong.

As the physically weak man can make himself strong by careful and patient training, so the man of weak thoughts can make them strong by exercising himself in right thinking. To put away aimlessness and weakness, and to begin to think with purpose, is to enter the ranks of those strong ones who only recognize failure as one of the pathways to attainment; who make all conditions serve them, and who think strongly, attempt fearlessly, and accomplish masterfully.

Having conceived of his purpose, a man should mentally mark out a *straight* pathway to its achievement, looking neither to the right nor to the left. Doubts and fears should be rigorously excluded, for they are disintegrating elements which break up the straight line of effort, rendering it crooked, ineffectual, useless. Thoughts of doubt and fear have never accomplished anything, and never will. They always lead to failure. Purpose, energy, power to do, and all strong thoughts cease when doubt and fear creep in.

The will to do springs from the knowledge that we *can* do. Doubt and fear are the great enemies of knowledge, and he who encourages them, who does not slay them, thwarts himself at every step. He who has conquered doubt and fear has conquered failure. His every thought is allied with power, and all difficulties are bravely met and wisely overcome. His purposes are seasonably planted, and they bloom and bring forth fruit which does not fall prematurely to the ground.

Thought allied fearlessly to purpose becomes

creative force. He who *knows* this is ready to become something higher and stronger than a mere bundle of wavering thoughts and fluctuating sensations. He who *does* this has become the conscious and intelligent wielder of his mental powers.

The
Thought-Factor
in Achievement

All that a man achieves and all that he fails
to achieve is the direct result of his own thoughts.
In a justly ordered universe, where loss of equi-
poise would mean total destruction, individual
responsibility must be absolute. A man's weakness and strength, purity and impurity, are his
own, and not another man's. They are brought
about by himself, and not by another; and they
can only be altered by himself, never by another. His condition is also his own, and not
another man's. His suffering and his happiness
are evolved from within. As he thinks, so he is.
As he continues to think, so he remains.

A strong man cannot help a weaker unless
that weaker is *willing* to be helped, and even
then the weak man must become strong of himself; he must, by his own efforts, develop the
strength which he admires in another. None but
himself can alter his condition.

It has been usual for men to think and say,

"Many men are slaves because one is an oppressor; let us hate the oppressor." Now however, there is, amongst an increasing few, a tendency to reverse this judgement, and to say, "One man is an oppressor because many are slaves; let us despise the slaves." The truth is that oppressor and slave are co-operators in ignorance, and, while seeming to afflict each other, are in reality afflicting themselves. A perfect Knowledge perceives the action of law in the weakness of the oppressed and the misapplied power of the oppressor. A perfect Love, seeing the suffering which both states entail condemns neither. A perfect Compassion embraces both oppressor and oppressed.

He who has conquered weakness, and has put away all selfish thoughts, belongs neither to oppressor nor oppressed. He is free.

A man can only rise, conquer, and achieve by lifting up his thoughts. He can only remain weak, and abject, and miserable, by refusing to lift up his thoughts.

Before a man can achieve anything, even in worldly things, he must lift his thoughts above slavish animal indulgence. He may not in order to succeed, give up *all* animality and selfishness, by any means; but a portion of it must, at least, be sacrificed. A man whose first thought is bestial indulgence could neither think clearly nor plan methodically. He could not find and develop his latent resources, and would fail in any undertaking. Not having commenced manfully to control his thoughts, he is not in a position to control affairs and to adopt serious responsibilities. He is not fit to act independently and stand alone. But he is limited only by the thoughts which he chooses.

There can be no progress, no achievement, without sacrifice. A man's worldly success will be in the measure that he sacrifices his confused, animal thoughts, and fixes his mind on the development of his plans, and the strengthening of his resolution and self-reliance. And the higher he lifts his thoughts, the more manly, upright, and righteous he becomes, the greater will be his success, the more blessed and enduring will be his achievements.

The universe does not favor the greedy, the dishonest, the vicious, although on the mere surface it may sometimes appear to do so. It helps the honest, the magnanimous, the virtuous. All the great teachers of the ages have declared this in varying forms, and to prove and know it, a man has but to persist in making himself more and more virtuous by lifting up his thoughts.

Intellectual achievements are the result of thought consecrated to the search for knowledge, or for the beautiful and true in life and nature. Such achievements may be sometimes connected with vanity and ambition, but they are not the outcome of those characteristics.

They are the natural outgrowth of long and arduous effort, and of pure and unselfish thoughts.

Spiritual achievements are the consummation of holy aspirations. He who lives constantly in the conception of noble and lofty thoughts, who dwells upon all that is pure and unselfish, will as surely as the sun reaches its zenith and the moon its full, become wise and noble in character, and rise into a position of influence and blessedness.

Achievement, of whatever kind, is the crown of effort, the diadem of thought. By the aid of self-control, resolution, purity, righteousness, and well-directed thought, a man ascends. By the aid of animality, indolence, impurity, corruption, and confusion of thought, a man descends.

A man may rise to high success in the world, and even lofty altitudes in the spiritual realm, and again descend into weakness and wretchedness by allowing arrogant, selfish, and corrupt thoughts to take possession of him. Victories attained by right thought can only be maintained by watchfulness. Many give way when success is assured, and rapidly fall back into failure.

All achievements, whether in the business, intellectual, or spiritual world, are the result of definitely directed thought. They are governed by the same law, and are of the same method. The only difference lies in *the object of attain-*

ment. He who would accomplish little must sacrifice little. He who would achieve much must sacrifice much. He who would attain highly must sacrifice greatly.

Visions and Ideals

The dreamers are the saviors of the world. As the visible world is sustained by the invisible, so men, through their trials and sins and sordid vocations, are nourished by the beautiful visions of solitary dreamers. Humanity cannot forget its dreamers. It cannot let their ideals fade and die. It lives in them; it knows them as the *realities* which it shall one day see and know.

Composer, sculptor, painter, poet, prophet, sage, these are the makers of the after-world, the architects of heaven. The world is beautiful because they have lived. Without them, laboring humanity would perish.

He who cherishes a beautiful vision, a lofty ideal in his heart, will one day realize it. Columbus cherished a vision of another world, and he discovered it. Copernicus fostered the vision of a multiplicity of worlds and a wider universe, and he revealed it. Buddha beheld the vision of a spiritual world of stainless beauty and perfect peace, and he entered into it.

Cherish your visions. Cherish your ideals. Cherish the music that stirs in your heart, the beauty that forms in your mind, the loveliness that drapes your purest thoughts; for out of them will grow all delightful conditions, all heavenly environment. Of these, if you but remain true to them, your world will at last be built.

To desire is to obtain. To aspire is to achieve. Shall man's basest desires receive the fullest measure of gratification, and his purest aspirations starve for lack of sustenance? Such is not the law. Such a condition of things can never obtain, "Ask and receive."

Dream lofty dreams, and as you dream, so shall you become. Your Vision is the promise of what you shall one day be. Your Ideal is the prophecy of what you shall at last unveil.

The greatest achievement was at first and for a time a mere dream. The oak sleeps in the acorn; the bird waits in the egg; and in the highest vision of the soul, a waking angel stirs. Dreams are the seedlings of realities.

Your circumstances may be uncongenial, but they shall not long remain so if you but perceive an Ideal and strive to reach it. You cannot travel *within* and stand still *without*. Here is a youth hard pressed by poverty and labor, confined long hours in an unhealthy workshop, unschooled, and lacking all the arts of refinement. But he dreams of better things. He thinks of intelligence, of refinement, of grace and beauty. He conceives of, mentally builds up, an ideal condition of life. The vision of a wider liberty takes possession of him. Unrest urges him to action, and he utilizes all his spare time and means, small though they are, to the development of his latent powers and resources. Very soon, so altered has his mind become, that the workshop can no longer hold him. It has become so out of harmony with his mentality that it falls out of his life as a garment is cast aside, and, with the growth of opportunities which fit the scope of his expanding powers, he passes out of it forever. Years later we see this youth as a full-grown man and the master of certain forces of the mind which he wields with world-wide influence and almost unequaled power. In his hands he holds the cords of gigantic responsibilities. He speaks, and lo! lives are changed. Men and woman hang upon his words remold their characters. Sunlike, he becomes the fixed and luminous center round which innumerable destinies revolve.

He has realized the Vision of his youth. He has become one with his Ideal.

And you, too, will realize the Vision (not the idle wish) of your heart, be it base or beautiful, or a mixture of both; for you will always gravitate toward that which you secretly love most. Into your hands will be placed the exact results of your own thoughts. You will receive that which you earn, no more, no less. Whatever your present environment may be, you will fall, remain, or rise with your thoughts, your Vision, your Ideal. You will become as small as your controlling desire, as great as your dominant aspiration. In the beautiful words of Stanton Kirkham Davis, "You may be keeing accounts, and presently you shall walk out of the door that for so long has seemed to you the barrier of your ideals, and shall find yourself before an audience—the pen still behind your ear, the inkstains on your fingers—and then and there shall pour out the torrent of your inspiration. You may be driving sheep, and you shall wander to the city—bucolic and open-mouthed, shall wander under the intrepid guidance of the spirit into the studio of the master, and after a time he shall say, 'I have nothing more to teach you.' And now you have become the master, who did so recently dream of great things while driving sheep. You shall lay down the saw and the plane to take upon yourself the regeneration of the world."

The thoughtless, the ignorant, and the indolent, seeing only the apparent effects of things and not the things themselves, talk of luck, of fortune, and chance. Seeing a man grow rich, they say, "How lucky he is!" Observing another become intellectual, they explain, "How highly favored he is!" And noting the saintly character and wide influence of another, they remark, "How chance aids him at every turn!" They do not see the trials and failures and struggles which these men have voluntarily encountered in order to gain their experience. They have no knowledge of the sacrifices they have made, of the undaunted efforts they have put forth, of the faith they have exercised, in order to overcome the apparently insurmountable, and realize the Vision of their heart. Nor do they know the darkness and the heartaches; they only see the light and joy, and call it "luck". They do not see the long and arduous journey, but only behold the pleasant goal, and call it "good fortune". Neither do they understand the process, but only perceive the result, and call it "chance".

In all human affairs there are *efforts,* and there are *results,* and the strength of the effort is the measure of the result. Chance is not. "Gifts," powers, material, intellectual and spiritual possessions are the fruits of effort; they are thoughts completed, objects accomplished, visions realized.

The Vision that you glorify in your mind, the Ideal that you enthrone in your heart—this you will build your life by, this you will become.

Serenity

Calmness of mind is one of the beautiful jewels of wisdom. It is the result of long and patient effort in self-control. Its presence is an indication of ripened experience, and of a more than ordinary knowledge of the laws and operations of thought.

A man becomes calm in the measure that he understands himself as a thought-evolved being; for such knowledge necessitates the understanding of others as the result of thought. As he develops a right understanding, and sees more and more clearly the internal relations of things by action of cause and effort, he ceases to fuss and fume and worry and grieve, and remains poised, steadfast, serene.

The calm man, having learned how to govern himself, knows how to adapt himself to others; and they, in turn, revere his spiritual strength, and feel they can learn from him and rely upon him. The more tranquil a man becomes, the greater is his success, his influence, his power for good. Even the ordinary trader will find his business prosperity increase as he develops a greater self-control and equanimity; for people will always prefer to deal with a man whose demeanor is strongly equable.

The strong, calm man is always loved and revered. He is like a shade-giving tree in a thirsty land, or a sheltering rock in a storm. Who does not love a tranquil heart, a sweet-tempered, balanced life? It does not matter whether it rains or shines, or what changes come to those possessing these blessings, for they are always sweet, serene, and calm. That exquisite poise of character which we call serenity is the last lesson of culture. It is the flowering of life, the fruitage of the soul. It is precious as wisdom. more to be desired than gold—yea, than even fine gold. How insignificant mere money-seeking looks in comparison with a serene life—a life that dwells in the ocean of Truth, beneath the waves, beyond the reach of tempests, in the Eternal Calm!

How many people we know who sour their lives, who ruin all that is sweet and beautiful by explosive tempers, who destroy their poise of character, and make bad blood! It is a question whether the great majority of people do not ruin their lives and mar their happiness by lack of self-control. How few people we meet in life who are well-balanced, who have that exquisite poise which is characteristic of the finished character!

Yes, humanity surges with uncontrolled passion, is tumultous with ungoverned grief, is blown about by anxiety and doubt. Only the wise man, only he whose thoughts are controlled and purified, makes the winds and the storms of the soul obey him.

Tempest-tossed souls, wherever ye may be, under whatever conditions ye may live, know this—in the ocean of life the isles of Blessedness are smiling, and the sunny shore of your ideal awaits your coming. Keep your hand firmly upon the helm of thought. In the barque of your soul reclines the commanding Master; He does but sleep. Wake Him. Self-control is strength. Right Thought is mastery. Calmness is power. Say unto you heart, "Peace, be still!"